Real Learning:
Education in the Heart of the Home

by Elizabeth Foss

Real Learning:
Education in the Heart of the Home
by Elizabeth Foss

ISBN 0-97188-951-1

©2003 By Way of the Family Press
Saint Paul, MN

Cover illustration by Stephen Rayment
Cover design and production by Debora Drower
Interior design by Chelsea Allan
Calligraphy p. 118 by Marta Garbarino of Give Glory Arts & Crafts
Children's art credits are given on p. 252

All rights reserved. No part of this publication may be reproduced or transmitted in any form or by any means, electronic or mechanical, including photocopy, recording, or any information storage and retrieval system, without the prior permission of the publisher except as provided by USA copyright law.

Printed in the United States of America

To my daughters, Mary Beth and Kirsten:
you have already taught me so much
that I know you will one day be wonderful teachers.

Table of Contents

Acknowledgments
[8]

Foreword by Melissa Wiley
[11]

A Foundation
[17]

Charlotte Mason and Beyond
[25]

Education Is an Atmosphere
[27]

Education Is a Discipline
[34]

Education Is a Life
[42]

The Art of Language Arts
[55]

Teaching Reading
[55]

Teaching Writing
[63]

Math with Meaning
[75]

Blowing the Dust off History and Science
[87]

History
[90]

Science
[94]

Religion: An Intimate Relationship with God
[119]

An Integrated Literature Unit
for Advent and Christmas
with Recipe Box
[131]

Creativity — Cultivating Color and Cacophony
[145]

Special Blessings
[167]

Sports: A School of Virtue
[175]

The Practical Side of Atmosphere:
Children, Chores, and Character
[187]

Conquering Clutter
[188]

Children and Chores
[190]

Atmosphere on the Bad Days
[194]

Battling Back from Burnout
[205]

A Final Thought: Educated by Our Intimacies
[227]

Read Around the Year Booklist
[231]

Children's Art Credits
[252]

Acknowledgments

Mothers of young children cannot write books alone. This book is fruit of the efforts and prayers of many, many people. I extend my heartfelt thanks to:

- The Lord of the Universe, Jesus Christ, with whom all things are possible.

- The Blessed Mother, without whose intercession I never would have found the time to write a book.

- Saint Teresa Benedicta (Edith Stein), Saint Francis of Assisi, and Saint Thomas Aquinas, whose constant intercession and inspiration have been guiding lights in this endeavor.

- MacBeth Derham, Linda McDonough, and Willa Ryan for thoughtful editing, the benefit of many philosophical conversations, your tireless work on the booklist, the treasure of the quotes you have unearthed, and mostly for your steadfast support and encouragement, your priceless friendship, and your prayers. I hope this book does justice to all of those.

- The women of Sursum Corda: Trisha Artigues, MacBeth Derham, Cindy Kelly, Willa Ryan, Michele Quigley, and Leonie Westenberg. We are educated by our intimacies, and I have learned so much from you. Thank you for sharing your wisdom. You have touched my heart and forever changed my soul.

- The women (and men) who have contributed so generously to the "Words from the Wise." I hope that you lift up the hearts of our readers as you have lifted mine.

- Barbara Rice, for insightful wisdom and comfortable friendship.

- Mary Hasson, my first homeschooling mentor, for your thoughtful editing, your wise counsel, and your invaluable inspiration.

- Melissa Peterson for the tangible encouragement and inspiration of a kindred spirit.

- Jennifer Hogan, for welcoming my children into your home and playing with them while I wrote in peace.

- Kate Kampa, for generously sharing your time and talent.

- Chelsea Allan, for being a thoughtful reader on the Catholic Charlotte Mason list who rescued this book and gently brought it to fruition.

- Bobby Convey, my spirited and charming soccer student, for allowing me to embark on a high-school home education adventure before my time. You, dear one, are part of the family.

- My father, who taught me, by his example, the power of a good book; and my mother, who turned off the television.

- My children, Stephen, Mary Beth, Patrick, Christian, and Michael, who prayed daily for "Mommy's Book," and Nicholas, who was with me for every word and thankfully stayed tucked up tight inside until the manuscript was in the mail.

- My son Michael, the one person without whom this book truly would not have been possible. You have done much dishwashing, laundry folding, sandwich making, and baby bouncing so that I would be free to write. I cannot begin to express how much I appreciate your cheerful cooperation.

- My husband, Mike, who left me "alone" to write far more than I would have liked. When I finished pouring myself into it, you took this project under your wing to deliver it safely to readers. This book, at its essence, is about you and me. It is the fruit of twenty years of late-night talks. It is our vision and, like our children, the fruit of our love. It is you who educates me, and it is your book as much as it is mine.

Foreword

by Melissa Wiley

My husband and I made the decision to homeschool our children when our oldest was just a baby. Like every other homeschooling mother I have met, I devoured shelves full of books on the subject and spent hours nibbling my way through the Internet's cornucopia of information. I read Holt, Gatto, Berquist, Hasson and Hahn. And somewhere along the way I had my first encounter with the phrase "living books."

Those words leapt off the page at me. Wasn't that what I had been doing my whole life — *living* books? Living in them, living with them, living through them. As a child I was so immersed in the worlds of Anne Shirley, Mary Lennox, Jo March, Lucy Pevensie, and most especially Laura Ingalls that it cost me tremendous effort to wrench myself back to the suburban classrooms of Aurora, Colorado. Laura's Plum Creek dugout and Anne's Lake of Shining Waters were places as vivid and real to me as my own home.

As an adult I went right on "living" books. Like my heroines Anne and Jo and Laura, I became a writer. In fact, in 1997 my lifelong affection for Laura Ingalls Wilder and her family led to a thrilling opportunity to research Laura's ancestors — her grandmother, Charlotte Tucker, and her Scottish great-grandmother, Martha Morse — and to write a series of novels about each of them. While writing *Little House by Boston Bay*, *Little House in the Highlands*, and other novels about Charlotte and Martha, I have truly lived and breathed and eaten with characters I hold very dear. My oldest daughter, now a chattering seven-year-old bookworm, even insists upon a passable Scottish brogue from me during the umpteen times a day I am called upon to "play" Martha.

The notion of giving my children an education based on "living books" was one that captured my heart and mind immediately. I began to search out books on the subject, and what I read delighted me. At the same time, I was searching for guidance in another aspect of child-rearing — one that, at the time, seemed separate from the question of how best to educate my children. I was a brand-new Catholic, having converted not long before my marriage, and as my daughter grew older I realized I had no idea what it meant to "raise a child in the Church." Of course I had my husband, a cradle Catholic, for guidance, but I wanted to know more; I wanted to know how best to live up to my parental calling to teach my children to know God, love Him, and serve Him.

One memorable day an Internet search engine turned up a website with the promising name of "Charlotte Mason in the Catholic Home." I knew vaguely that Charlotte Mason was a person who had written a great deal on the subject of using living books as the basis of a child's education. Living books and the Catholic home — this was a website I had to see. Eagerly I clicked, and the lives of every member of my household were forever changed.

The Catholic Charlotte Mason website was a treasure trove of articles by a homeschooling mother and writer named Elizabeth Foss. Each article was steeped in the conviction that the living-books method of home education allows enthusiastic learning to go hand in hand with sanctified living. Here were answers to my two most burning questions: how best to educate my children, and how to raise saints. I read hungrily; I downloaded and printed out; I joined the site's discussion group and spent months quietly soaking in the advice and experiences of women like Elizabeth Foss, Michele Quigley, MacBeth Derham, and Willa Ryan. I went through a comical amount of paper making copies of choice articles and posts for the other mothers in my local Catholic homeschooling group.

I even stumbled upon a number of articles by Elizabeth Foss in the EWTN website's document library, articles which quickly confirmed my suspicions that here was a person whose ideas would bring blessings to my life. A devout and thoughtful Catholic, a gifted writer, an inspired homeschooler, and a devoted and cheerful mother — like my old pal Laura Ingalls Wilder, here was a woman whose writing had spoken to me like a friend.

I had but one criticism of Elizabeth: her insights were wearing out my computer. All those scattered slips of paper I was accumulating, all those hard-drive files of saved posts! *If only*, I often muttered in the kind of wishful thinking that is really a prayer, *if only all of this wisdom could be collected in one place. Elizabeth Foss should really write a book.*

I must not have been the only person making that prayer. Elizabeth has written that book. *This* book. It is a book so rich in ideas that as I read it, I could hardly restrain myself from leaping up every five minutes to implement them. It is a book both inspiring and practical, encompassing every aspect of the homeschooling life, from art, science, and history to religion, housekeeping, and athletics.

It is a book that fills me with humility and hope, for I have taken away from its pages a deeper understanding of my vocation as wife, mother, and homeschooler. Elizabeth Foss, with her profound love of her subject and her family and her Lord, has given us a moving, breathing, singing book — a book that will show you how to create within your home an atmosphere of joyful, constant learning with Christ at its center.

This, too, is a living book; and my life is better for having read it.

Melissa Wiley
July 2002
Crozet, Virginia

Join us on a journey through
Real Learning:
Education in the Heart of the Home.
Herein we have provided you
with a taste of real learning.
Several home-educated children
have graciously shared with us excerpts and samples
from nature journals, and art notebooks,
as well as drawings made especially for this book.
You will find them throughout the following chapters.
Art credits can be found at the end of the book.
Enjoy!

A Foundation

Did you ever have a teacher who set you on fire? He or she sparked in you an enthusiasm for the subject taught that burned so brightly you couldn't wait to learn more. I did. My third year in college, I was privileged to have two such teachers.

The first taught my classes in reading and writing instruction and reading disabilities. She was animated and enthusiastic. She talked about how children needed to learn to read in the context of whole books, and how they needed to read and to be read good literature every day. She urged us to abandon the senseless basal readers and to light fires in our young students. She covered phonics too, for about three class sessions. Phonics was a means to an end, and the end was reading for meaning.

She taught us that anything could be taught in the context of a good book, whether the subject matter was science or history or geography. She taught us that subjects were interrelated and that students' learning was more effective if they made those connections. I remember thinking that if she had been my elementary school teacher, I would have loved school. Instead of constantly being told to pull my nose out of a book and do my work, the book would have been my work.

The second teacher and I got off to a terrible start, or so I thought. He was new to the university and had been invited to guest lecture in one of my educational philosophy classes. His philosophy was entirely opposed to that which I had learned. I was utterly confused. If one professor said one thing and another said something else, then what was the right answer for the test? We were required to write a response paper, and I gave voice to my frustration. The professor scrawled across my paper, "I am not paid to agree with Professor X, I am paid to think for myself. You, too, can think for yourself."

I was intrigued. Think for myself. I was a college junior, nineteen years old, on the fast track to graduate with honors, and this was a novel idea. I had gotten where I was by knowing the right answer and taking tests well. Nobody had ever told me to think for myself before!

The following year, I was granted permission to do an independent study project under the guidance of the second teacher. I spent the semester researching British primary schools. There, I discovered Charlotte Mason — though not in her original writings. In all my reading I don't think I ever encountered her name. But I met her ideas. Her influence was woven throughout theories of education that I found fascinating. I wanted to provide for my students such things as a living books education, free from "twaddle." I liked the ideas of short lessons, no homework, free afternoons for nature study, and exposure to great artists, composers, and poets. I wanted to present great ideas and stand back, employing what Miss Mason calls "masterly inactivity" while my students formed relationships with the ideas. I wanted them to know, when they were four or six or eight, and well before they were nineteen, that they could and should think for themselves.

Then I got a job in the public schools. I was ordered to stick to the Program of Study and the Standards of Learning objectives. Every child was to go through the same program. They were all to be on the same page in math at the same time. And they were all to read every single basal reader in order and do all the workbook pages.

My first graders were from very poor homes. These children rarely came to school with a full stomach, and most had never been read to at home. What they needed most to further their education was a lap, a good book, and someone to read to them. I was terribly frustrated that year. I was also pregnant. And I promised myself that no child of mine would ever sit in a stifling classroom.

I had seen institutionalized education from both sides of the desk, and I knew that I wanted none of it for my children.

That was the year the Colfaxes, a family in California, were becoming famous for their innovative educational theories. They were educating their children at home, and their children were going to Harvard and Oxford and doing wonderfully well. The Colfaxes wrote a book, *Homeschooling for Excellence*.

When I went to buy the book, I noticed another on the shelf: *For the Children's Sake* by Susan Schaeffer MacCauley. I bought them both. The Colfaxes inspired me

with their reports of educating with real books and real life experiences. MacCauley inspired me with the ideas of Charlotte Mason. At last, someone had written down what I wanted for my children: an education that drew on living books, real life experiences, great art and music.

    I have read a great many books on home education since I first read those by the Colfaxes and MacCauley. And I have noticed that there is a great diversity in goals even among home educators. Some educators' primary goal appears to be preparing a child for a certain college experience. Some concentrate on character development and leave the academics entirely to textbooks and workbooks. Some parents are "homeschooling," as an endeavor to bring a Catholic school experience to the dining-room table. This book is not about "homeschooling" at all. School is an artificial institution contrived by man. This book is about educating a child in the heart of the family given to that child by his Creator. It is not about school at home — it is about something better.

We must be very clear about our goals in education if we are to educate well. What does it mean to be educated? In the school where I taught, it meant pouring facts into a child's head so the child could take a test and move on to more facts. It was focused upon measurable quantities of information and retention of information. This segmenting of education, the idea that education can be broken down and compartmentalized, is the prevailing notion. Children are considered buckets to be filled. Education is merely the imparting of certain facts and skills over time. Consider, instead, Charlotte Mason's vision of education:

> *The idea that vivifies teaching…is that 'Education is a Science of Relations;' by which phrase we mean that children come into the world with a natural [appetite] for, and affinity with, all the material of knowledge; for interest in the heroic past and in the age of myths; for a desire to know about everything that moves and lives, about strange places and strange peoples; for a wish to handle material and to make; a desire to run and ride and row and do whatever the law of gravitation permits. Therefore…we endeavor that he shall have relations of pleasure and intimacy established with as many possible of the interests proper to him; not learning a slight or incomplete smattering about this or that subject, but plunging into vital knowledge, with a great field before him which in all his life he will not be able to explore. In the conception we get that 'touch of emotion' which vivifies knowledge, for it is probable that we feel only as we are brought into our proper vital relations.* (School Education, 222–223)

It wasn't until I had been educating my children at home for several years that the final piece fell into the puzzle. Education at home works so well because parent educators naturally dedicate their hearts and souls to touching the hearts and souls of their children. This vision, a fresh vision of education and of the child, has been greatly influenced by the writings of Saint Teresa Benedicta, the German Carmelite nun who was born Edith Stein. In her writing, I hear echoes of Miss Mason, though I doubt she ever read any of Charlotte Mason's books. Both women emphasize the absolute necessity of engaging the whole child — heart, soul, and mind — in order to educate him.

Edith Stein writes, "God's image is like a seed planted in the human soul. In order to bring this inner form to development, the human creature needs formative help of two sorts: the supernatural aid of grace and the natural help of the human educational process…This full development of personality implies a wholeness of personality because it is the whole person that is needed for God's service. If pupils receive this help, they can by an inner dedication become more similar to the inborn ideal image [that God has intended]." (*Woman*, 8)

Again and again we see the truth that each child is created to reflect God's image in a unique way. A child's personality and personhood is God-given. We can't and shouldn't try to make a child into "our own image" or into what we think he should be, or what some curriculum designer thinks he should be. It is the role of parent and educator to help a child become more like the "ideal image" that God has in mind for him. To bring about this ideal in our children involves three forces: the supernatural aid of grace; the human educational process; and the student's dedication to the process.

Throughout a child's lifetime, in our vocation as parent educators, we will be brought to our knees, praying for God's direction for our children and our families. As we seek direction, we will also teach our children to seek divine direction. Edith Stein was a staunch advocate for the principle that religious education is at the heart of all education.

Educating a child's mind is a primary goal of home education and is absolutely essential to helping our children become what God wants them to be. Edith Stein believed in balanced formation — the heart, soul, and mind all need to be educated. She was a strong critic of the education system of her day which stressed memorization and the acquisition of unrelated facts. Charlotte Mason concurs when she writes, "Upon the knowledge of these great matters — History, Literature, Nature, Science, Art — the Mind feeds and grows. It assimilates such knowledge as the body assimilates food, and the person becomes what is called magnanimous — that is a person of great mind, wide interests, incapable of occupying himself much about petty, personal matters. What a pity to lose sight of such a possibility for the sake of miserable scraps of information about persons and things that have little connection with one another and little connection with ourselves!" (*Ourselves*, 78)

Edith Stein deplored the fact that the idea of education typically is "that of encyclopedic knowledge: the presumed concept of the mind [is] that of the *tabula rasa* onto which as many impressions as possible [are] to be registered through intellectual perceptions and memorizations." (*Woman*, 130) Like Charlotte Mason, she recognized that education is so much more than the acquisition of encyclopedic knowledge. In the poetic words of William Butler Yeats, "Education is not filling a bucket, but lighting a fire."

Edith Stein wrote that the teacher's job was to encourage the student's "inner participation" in the educational process. She was to get the student excited about the material, encourage a response, offer guidance, but ultimately the child was to make it his own. "The teacher's role in the formation of the students is an indirect one since all development is self-development. All training is self-training." (*Woman*, 5)

With these three forces in mind, we can look at a new paradigm for home education, one which focuses upon developing the whole personality of the child — the heart, soul, and mind — using the wisdom of Edith Stein and Charlotte Mason to pursue a happy, wholehearted, academically excellent, spiritually complete childhood.

Over and over again, both Edith Stein and Charlotte Mason articulate beautifully the need to reach a child's heart in order to truly educate him. We cannot limit education to that which is poured into a child's brain. Instead, we seek to touch the core of the child. Stein writes, "Actual formative material is received not merely by the senses and intellect but is integrated by the 'heart and soul' as well. But if it actually becomes transformed into the soul, then it ceases to be mere material: it works itself, forming, developing; it helps the soul to reach its intended gestalt." (*Woman*, 131)

I don't consider education from the perspective of filling buckets because I don't consider children from that perspective. When I look at a child, I see a living, breathing person, made in God's image, for whom God has a plan. As parent educators, we need to embrace a new notion of learning. We need to help the child discern the Lord's will and equip him to answer his particular call. It is the heart and soul of the child we want to touch. For our purposes, we need to engage the heart in order to effectively educate the child. Our vision of a well-educated child is a child who has a heart for learning, a child who has the tools he needs to continue to learn for a lifetime and a child who has the love to want to do it. He has been led to a lifetime of learning all the time.

We must be absolutely certain of our goals in education. When we know where we are going, we can confidently chart our course. We want children who know, love, and serve the Lord. As their primary educators, it is our privilege and our duty to equip them for that task.

I want my children to love learning. I want them to revel in their curiosity and delight in their discoveries. And I want to learn alongside them.

As a child, I detested math. I didn't understand it and I tended to avoid it. Watching my boys "play with numbers," I have a new appreciation for math. Through their eyes, I can see the orderliness of the systems and the meaning of the patterns. It's almost fun. I can see that even math is a blessing.

Math is perfectly ordered by God. It is not difficult to see the perfect hand of the Creator in the science of mathematics. It is even simpler to see His hand in art and literature, poetry and music, and the infinite beauty of nature. God is there. He wants us to know Him there, and He wants our children to know Him, too. He cannot be confined to the pages of a textbook. He cannot be trapped in a box shipped from a curriculum supplier. He is bigger than that. He is Life. And He wants us to have that life abundantly.

Charlotte Mason and Beyond

Charlotte Mason was a British woman of the last century who founded the House of Education in Ambleside, England, in the beautiful Lake District. She was born in 1842, an Anglican woman and a pioneer in educational reform. She founded the Parents National Educational Union (PNEU), perhaps the first homeschool support group ever. She also published the *Parent's Review*, a periodical written to guide parents who were educating children at home.

She seemed to love mottoes, and her motto for the parents of PNEU was: "Education is an atmosphere, a discipline, and a life." She wrote volumes about the three educational instruments: the atmosphere of environment, the discipline of habit, and the presentation of living ideas.

It was Miss Mason's belief that children are educated by their intimacies. Karen Andreola writes,

> *We, as persons, are not enlightened by means of multiple-choice tests or grades, but rather by the other people in our lives that we come to know, admire, and love. We are educated by our friendships and by our intimacies. For instance, think how the actions of someone you admire influence your behavior. Similarly, think also of how a boy's interest is sparked by a hobby he loves, and to which he devotes all his time and trouble. Whether it be gardening, keeping house, or governing a state, love of work — like love of people — teaches things that no school, no system can. (A Charlotte Mason Companion, 23)*

 The goal of such an education is to surround the child with noble people and books and other things with which to form relationships. For a Catholic parent, the first intimacy we want for our children is a true personal friendship with the Lord. All our educating is directed to that end.

 We also recognize that the child living in a home that is also his "school" will form very close relationships with his parents and siblings. It is these relationships that we pray about unceasingly. We endeavor to be good examples and mentors. We want strong, loving bonds between siblings. Despite our inadequacies, we strive in our homes to emulate the Holy Family.

 The child will also have intimacies with literature and nature and music and art. With an eye toward the ultimate goal, only the finest of these are set before the child. Children need the time and space to meet fine ideas and to make them their own. The atmosphere of the home and, indeed, of the child's entire environment can be ordered toward the purpose of presenting living ideas.

Education Is an Atmosphere

When Charlotte Mason said that education is an atmosphere, she did not mean that "a child should be isolated in what may be called a child environment, especially adapted and prepared, but that we should take into account the educational value of his natural home atmosphere, both as regards persons and things, and should let him live freely among his proper conditions."

For most children, a home environment is all they need to thrive. Of course, we will adapt that home environment so that both big people and little ones can live there. Many preschool and kindergarten classrooms in the United States endeavor to create the perfect "child-centered" atmosphere where everything is artificially arranged for the child. They have been heavily influenced by the work of Maria Montessori. We don't need to re-create kindergartens in our homes. While we certainly want homes where the child is comfortable and welcome, children thrive in "real" homes where adults and children both live.

We can borrow from much of Maria Montessori's thought as we design our own philosophy of education. We can look to provide beautiful, natural, high-quality playthings for our children, but we need not embrace the entire Montessori program in our homes, or duplicate the very specific, expensive materials. *At Home with Montessori* by Patricia Oriti is a lovely illustrated little book that makes the Montessori approach to environment a practical one at home. This book is entirely compatible with Charlotte Mason. However, in an effort to provide the very best of all that is available, don't limit your thought on atmosphere to Maria Montessori. Look to Charlotte Mason as well. Atmosphere is so much more than furniture arrangement and accessibility of supplies.

Think about the atmosphere in your home. Are you struggling through a lean financial time? Are you rejoicing in the birth of a baby? Are you mourning the loss of a grandparent? Are you moving across the country? This is the atmosphere God has given you, and it is the atmosphere in which He wants you to raise your children. First and foremost, it must be an atmosphere of faith.

Willa Ryan, writing from San Francisco, where she, her husband, and five children are living temporarily to be near her infant son who is awaiting a liver transplant, shares:

Right now our family is in a state of crisis. We are defined at least in part by what we do not have. We do not have our house, we do not have our baby, we do not have the books and materials we have accumulated over several years. Nothing is status quo right now. The children have watched more junky TV and eaten more hot dogs in the past two months than they have in the previous two years. The ideal Charlotte Mason education and the ideal Charlotte Mason educator seem as far away as the moon. So once again, what is our goal in homeschooling? What do we have when everything else is gone? I'm still trying to figure that out, with a lot of tears and prayers and good resolutions that don't always go anywhere. But here's what I do know…if we are homeschooling our children because we want to raise saints we can take comfort in the fact that God blesses us in our deprivations as well as in our abundances.

Or rather, our very abundances of His grace can come from our deprivations. It's easier for me to write about these things than to live as if they were true. Undergoing sorrow doesn't necessarily bestow an automatic halo on a family. My children are displaying characteristics of hostility and selfishness. And why shouldn't they? Their mother is displaying the same characteristics! So, since my children and I are so far from my ideal at the moment, should I give up on homeschooling and the whole Charlotte Mason philosophy, and send the children to school? Well, my husband and I considered it but not for very long. It didn't take us long to realize that if homeschooling is right for us when we are blessed with abundances of health, good living circumstances, and amiable tendencies, it must still be right for us when these things are taken away. As parents, we are called on to be generous in bringing children into the world and also to be responsible and diligent in raising them in the faith. Parents sanctify their children, but children also sanctify their parents.

A family is uniquely suited to sanctify its members — it's a refining process, burning away the dross and preserving the gold. Dross can give off an ugly smell as it burns away, but that is better than trying to bury or hide it in the hope that it will go away. That's why I am homeschooling. Because I want our family to meet in heaven someday, and I think we have a better shot at it if we journey together as much as possible. God put us together for a reason. Because I think even a tired, sorrowful, preoccupied mom and dad are better for their children than the best teachers in the best school. And that when my children show character flaws that I am not sure how to deal with because I have the same flaws, that God would rather have me battle them out in my inadequate way, asking for His grace and provision, than rely on outside solutions (like sending them to school) to solve the problems. Homeschooling brings many abundances and consolations, but some of the abundances are disguised as pain. And that's what a real Catholic life must look like, for Jesus says, "A seed must die to bear fruit."

We set out to create an atmosphere that encourages learning and growing in faith. As Willa points out, it is not always ideal. Certainly, we endeavor to affect that atmosphere by filling it with whatsoever is good, desirable, and of good report. I want to create in my home an atmosphere for what the author Sally Clarkson calls "home-centered learning." That is, I want to deliberately create an environment where children learn even if I am not actively teaching. It is true that I want this environment to be beautiful, but my goals go beyond beauty.

In Charlotte Mason's day, children were not highly valued. Poor children worked under terrible conditions. Rich children were raised by governesses and closeted in nurseries out of the way of their parents. Today, children are murdered in what God intended as the perfect place to grow, their mother's womb. Or they are born to be all but abandoned in daycare institutions and robbed of their childhood by a materialistic culture.

I know a six-year-old child who lives in a million-dollar home. The house is beautifully decorated, down to the last little detail. It looks like a model home in *House Beautiful.* The only books in sight are those whose dust jackets match the decor. There are no dolls, no dress-up clothes, no kitchen toys. Her mother says they are clutter, and the child is entertained by the computer and Nintendo video games. She attends kindergarten all day and then she has all sorts of lessons after school. They are not home very much.

The child in my example is as deprived as those impoverished children in my first classroom. Consider, instead of that model perfect home, one which is bursting with beauty and with ideas. It may not be as big and it is almost certainly messier than the *House Beautiful* home, but there is a lot of learning going on there. There is a learning room full of things that foster creativity: LEGO building bricks, Playmobil figures, dress-up clothes, paints, paper, writing and editing programs on the computer, dolls, blocks, and books, lots and lots of books.

Studies have shown that the more books in a child's home the more likely that the child will be intelligent. The books in this home are not confined to the learning room but are easily available in every room in the house. They are in baskets in the family room, the living room, and the bathroom. They are on bedside tables, in bags to take to the pool, and on tapes in the car. And they are not the dumbed-down, insipid books that Charlotte Mason would call "twaddle." They are books of high moral quality, full of worthy ideas and fine language. They are living books.

They are the core of the children's education in this home. Textbooks are used rarely and only for reference.

What is the difference between textbooks and living books?

Clay and Sally Clarkson, in their excellent, absolutely indispensable book *Educating the WholeHearted Child*, compare textbooks with living books:

- *A living book is written by a single author, a real and knowable person.*
- *A textbook is written by various authors or contributors, usually unknown.*
- *A living book is a literary expression of the author's own ideas and love of the subject.*
- *A textbook is a non-literary expression of collected facts and information.*
- *A living book is personal in tone and feel. It touches the heart and emotions, and the intellect.*
- *A textbook is impersonal in tone and feel. It touches only the intellect.*
- *The author of a living book addresses the reader as an intelligent and capable thinker.*
- *In a living book, ideas are presented creatively in a way that stimulates the imagination.*
- *In a textbook, facts are presented without creativity in a way that deadens the imagination.*

(*Educating the WholeHearted Child*, 80)

The atmosphere of the home we are considering is alive with living books and living ideas. There are art books and prints of works by the great masters. There is a garden, however small, where wee hands are invited and encouraged to touch, to feel, and to grow. And every afternoon, at four o'clock, there is teatime. Flowers on the table, Mozart on the CD player and a goodie or two on the table. The children are seated around the table where they are given the undivided attention of their mother and encouraged to talk; to discuss and to relate living ideas; to celebrate the feasts of the liturgical year. That is the atmosphere of education.

One summer I learned in a tangible way that children are often products of their environment. We had a child from Belfast living with us. He was eleven years old. He arrived during a ferocious heat wave. One afternoon, I pulled all the shades and suggested to the boys that they read quietly for awhile. My ten-year-old walked slowly to his room, his nose already buried in a book, his mind far from me in Redwall Abbey.

My visitor followed more slowly and paced in front of the bookshelves.

"Don't you read?" I asked him.

"No," he replied.

"Never?" said I.

"No."

"What do you do for school?" my seven-year-old asked incredulously.

Our visitor shrugged, and I, at a complete loss, whisked him out of the room to play Amazon Trail on the computer.

When I related the story to my husband, he suggested that maybe he didn't know how to read. Oh, so that's why God put him in our house. I'll just teach him how. So I began another series of questions:

"The other day, you said you don't read. Does that mean that you don't like to read or you don't know how?"

"Don't know how."

"Before Michael was born, I was a reading teacher. I could teach you to read this summer. Would you like that?"

"No."

"You don't want to know how to read?"

"No."

Again, I was at a loss for words. This was a child who had probably never been read to. He was never presented with great ideas. When he arrived at our house he would sit and do nothing for hours each day, at a loss without either a soccer ball or a television. His education had never touched his heart.

Given a summer, I could have taught him to read. He could have left my home with a solid phonics education. But could I teach him to want to read? Could I instill in him a love of books, a desire to have and hold dear that which is held between the covers of a book? One thing is certain: I couldn't begin to do that sitting at the table with a workbook open in front of us.

That day, I suggested a nature walk. Before we could go, my two-year-old daughter came inside with a nice big beetle in her bug box. Our visitor was fascinated.

"What is it?" I asked. "What do they do? Are they good for the garden, or should we be concerned?"

Out came the field guides, which we keep close at hand for times such as these. The poor little bug was scrutinized, identified, sketched, and carried far, far away from Mom's precious plants. Our visitor was flushed with excitement. His learning was ignited by his delight and fed by his atmosphere.

And all I did was ask three questions. Charlotte Mason encouraged her teachers to prudently exercise "masterly inactivity." Edith Stein writes, "As long as the teacher succeeds in stimulating the student's receptivity, as a person he recedes more and more into the background." (*Woman*, 9)

Present the ideas, provide the resources, and get out of the way. When the atmosphere encourages learning, the learning is inevitable.

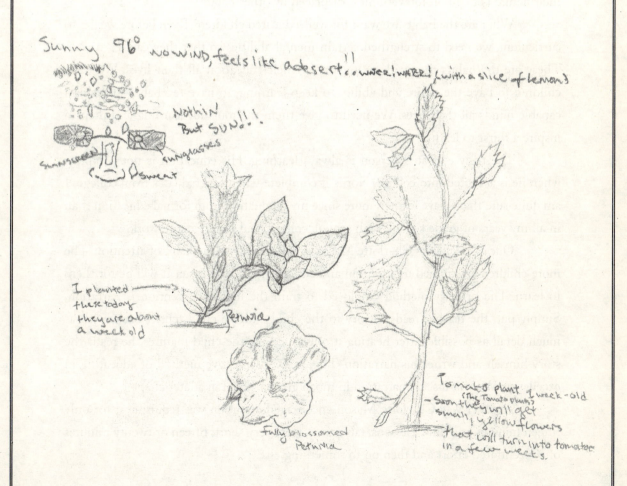

Education Is a Discipline

Charlotte Mason believed that one-third of education was discipline. She wrote: "By 'education is a discipline' is meant the discipline of habits formed definitely and thoughtfully whether habits of mind or body. Physiologists tell us of the adaptation of brain structure to habitual lines of thoughts. That is, to our habits. We run our lives on the tracks laid down by habit." She said, "actual confirmation of the child's brain depends upon the habits that the parents permit or encourage and that the habits of the child produce the character of the man because certain mental habitudes, once set up, their nature is to go on forever unless displaced by other habits."

What are the habits we want for well-educated children? Even before we get to curriculum, we need to strengthen certain mental abilities so that they can learn well. These are the habits they will use to further their education all their lives. We want children to have the desire and ability to keep learning, to have teachable spirits and capable minds all their lives. We need to give them the tools for learning and then to inspire a thirst to learn.

The truly educated person is always learning. His education is not complete when he is accepted into college. Nor is it complete when he graduates from college. I am quite sure that I have learned more since my graduation from formal education than in all my years of grade school, high school, college, and postgraduate work.

One of the habits Charlotte Mason emphasized was the habit of attention. The more children are trained in attention and concentration, the easier it will be for them to learn. The primary method employed to train the habit of attention is narration. Simply put, the teacher reads a story to the child and the child tells it back, with as much detail as possible, after hearing it only once. As the child matures, he reads the story himself and writes his narration. This is a very effective method of educating in excellence. We will discuss narration in much greater detail in a later chapter.

Another way Charlotte Mason encouraged attention was requiring it for only fifteen minutes at a time. Lessons, table time, were very short: fifteen or twenty minutes of concentrated effort and then on to something else.

What about the habit of inquisitiveness? Curiosity? Children are naturally curious. It is simply up to us to nurture that curiosity. Did you know that the average four-year-old asks one hundred questions a day? I wonder how many questions the average forty-year-old asks. We want them to keep asking. Bishop Mandell Creighton writes, "The one real object of education is to have a man in the condition of continually asking questions." We want children to wonder and to find out, "Why?" Let them explore their environment. Let them mess around in the kitchen or the workshop. Give them mechanical things to take apart and put together.

Consider the habit of orderliness and neatness: some children are naturally more inclined to neatness, but all need to mature. We can all grow in orderliness. Chores are an integral part of the home-education lifestyle, both for mother and child. Household management is often the place where a mother will begin training herself in good habits.

Interestingly enough, the child can discover order in the natural world. Karen Andreola, in her lovely book, *A Charlotte Mason Companion*, describes how a chipmunk's burrow is perfectly ordered and how a child is inspired by the animal's example. Charlotte Mason wanted children to have an intimate relationship with nature. The entire elementary science curriculum revolves around nature walks and the keeping of nature journals. These journals, neat catalogs of careful observations, are a joy to behold and a source of lasting pride and joy for the child who creates them.

Another way to train the habit of observation is through picture study. Children are presented with prints of the great masters. Generally, the prints are presented one artist at a time, one print a week. The child has time to observe each print in great detail and to become intimately acquainted with the work. Charlotte Mason called this "picture study," and we will explore it further in a later chapter.

We cannot leave a discussion of discipline without briefly touching upon Charlotte Mason's views on training the will of the child. Notice that I did not write: "breaking the will," I wrote: "training the will." Just as the parents had a motto, so did the children. Their motto was: *I am, I can, I ought, I will.*

I am: When I was an education student I learned much that was worthwhile. I also learned much that was not. One graduate class I took was called "Affective Education." For an entire semester, we had "group discussions" about self-esteem. Children who are educated in Catholic homes according to the principles of Charlotte

Mason have no need of modern education's self-esteem verbiage. Instead, they come, with genuine humility, to the foot of the cross where hangs Jesus, the great "I Am." In the domestic church, the child learns that he matters, that he has worth, because the Son of God laid down His life to save that child's soul. He knows he was created to know, love, and serve the Lord in this life and to live with Him forever in heaven. He knows that he was created in the image of the Creator and nothing more need be said about self-esteem.

This sense of the child as a creation of the Lord must permeate every aspect of our planning for his education. The parent educator must ask the Lord again and again, "Who is this child? For what have You created him? How can I equip him to answer Your call?" It is in asking these questions, and in teaching the child to ask these questions and to listen to the answers, that he learns to say with confidence: "I am."

I can: The child learns through experience that he is capable. He also learns that he will fail. He learns that he can do all things through Christ who strengthens him. And he learns it in the safety of a secure learning home. He learns that he will fall and learns the beauty of confession and forgiveness.

The parent educator enables the child to say, "I can," when she is sensitive to his interests and his abilities. She scatters great ideas along the landscape of his world and inspires him to interact with them as he is able. An effective educator will be sensitive to both his abilities and his limitations. Instead of pushing him to work harder at those things to which he is not naturally inclined, she will strive for competency in those areas and focus on spending large amounts of time pursuing his gifts. The parent is so in tune with the child that she understands how to tailor his education to him in a unique way.

Edith Stein elaborates: "Ideally, the educator needs to adapt his concept of the harmonious person to the personality of the individual student, i.e., to visualize clearly the image that is suitable to the inner form of the student entrusted to him" (*Woman*, 10). In this atmosphere, the child is enabled to answer, "I can!" to the requirements of his education.

I ought: This habit is about duty. It is the habit of control, doing what is right because it is right. Children need to learn to focus on God's will, not their own and on a Spirit-inspired control, *not* a self-control. It is easy to be controlled by one's self. It is hard to die to one's self and live for God. The Holy Spirit will inspire, lead, and give strength and wisdom to the child who is taught to listen to the whispers of his God. This Spirit-inspired control enables children to do work — to finish their chores, to learn diligently, to volunteer reliably, and to stick to a marriage even when it is hard. They can do their duty. They can answer their call. They can control their tempers, their anger. They can work a little harder. "I ought" is enabled by "I will."

I will: Again and again, I hear that home education is not working because children won't obey. Mom can't get them to do the work. Frequently, this admission is followed by the belief that a canned curriculum will solve the problem. I assure you, it will not. The problem is discipline. And you're not going to like this, but the first problem is Mom's self-discipline. We must discipline ourselves to plan and follow through. We must discipline ourselves to be orderly. We must discipline ourselves to "do everything without complaining." And then we must discipline ourselves to discipline our children. The most important thing we do as educators is to form the character of our children. Undisciplined children ruin the atmosphere of the home and make everyone miserable. What's worse, they grow into undisciplined adults who are crippled by their inability to function as mature adults.

Consider the following exchange in my house:

"Patrick, pick up your socks and put them in the hamper."

"Why?" questions my miniature soccer star as he kicks the socks across the room.

"Because I'm the Mommy and I asked you to," I reply firmly.

Glad to help my cause, my five-year-old daughter begins singing exuberantly: "O-B-E-Y! Obey your mom and dad! O-B-E-Y it makes 'em very glad. Listen to the words they say. Obey your parents every day!"

There was a time when I would have explained that the socks need to be in the hamper in order for them to get to the washer and dryer so that they would get clean and he could wear them again. But I am quite certain Patrick knows and understands the laundry system in our house. So I get to the heart of the matter. His heart. So much of child-rearing is character training, and little children need to learn to obey. They need to be trained to answer affirmatively to authority.

We require obedience. We insist on obedience, and we work day after day, every single day, to ensure obedience. When we ask a child to do something, we are polite. But we are firm. We embrace the fact that we are in authority over our children. God put us there, and our children need us there. We teach them truth. We teach them that

God's laws are absolute, and we require them to obey those absolute laws. For a child, the first law is "Children, obey your parents in the Lord." The only reason we need to give our children is: For this is right. God says so. We don't shrink from our authoritative role. Rather, we see it as a gift.

Charlotte Mason writes, "Authority is not only a gift but a grace…Authority is that aspect of love which parents present to their children; parents know it is love, because to them it means continual self-denial, self-repression, self-sacrifice: children recognize it as love, because to them it means quiet rest and gaiety of heart. Perhaps the best aid to the maintenance of authority in the home is for those in authority to ask themselves daily that question which was presumptuously put to our Lord — 'Who gave thee this authority?'" (*School Education*, 24)

Of course, God did. And by golly, we had better be grateful good stewards of that gift. Let's unpack the quote a little. To train our children, we must deny ourselves. We can't administer occasional bursts of punishment and expect a good result. We must instead be incessantly watchful, patiently forming and preserving good habits. This means we are attentive and active. Those are habits to cultivate in ourselves.

To rid ourselves of bad habits, Charlotte Mason suggests we replace them with virtuous ones. I know that in my house, my children misbehave a good deal when I have been on the phone or in front of the computer too much. They misbehave when routines slack off and meals are not given enough thought. They misbehave when bedtime isn't observed or they are overprogrammed and too busy. They misbehave when I am inattentive or lazy or tired or inconsistent. Those are bad habits. I must consciously replace them with attention and diligence and action and consistent sleep.

Children recognize the Biblical living of our authority as love because it *is* love. Children who consistently misbehave are begging for moral guidance and a strong anchor. They are crying (or whining, as the case may be) for someone to be in authority. As they grow, the real tangible relationship with the authority that is the parent flowers into a full-blown relationship with God and an eager willingness to obey Him when they are adults.

The life of an adult Christian is not easy. You can expect that as you train your children for that life, there will be some unhappiness. But that unhappiness is nothing compared to the quiet rest and joyful peace that comes with being right with God.

Parents always ask how to make a child obey. First, we don't want blind obedience; we want the child to be inspired to obey because he believes it is right. We want virtuous obedience. We want to train the habit of control, doing what is right because it is right. Children need to learn to focus on God's will, not their own and on a Spirit-inspired control, *not* a self-control. Remember, a mature adult will die to self and be controlled by the Lord. We are training our children to become mature adults.

I do not agree with authors who think we need to spank the will into submission. I do not agree with those who suggest that every desirable behavior be correlated to star charts and complicated reward systems. I'm not a big fan of "time-out." Usually, a child who is misbehaving needs more of his parent's attention. He doesn't need to be sent away unless it's for a very short moment where both child and parent cool off before meeting to discuss and remedy the situation. And I do not agree with the experts who suggest we pinch our child so hard that the strong-willed child becomes weak. We *want* strong-willed children. That's right: children who give in to their own whims and desires are actually weak-willed. They need strength training. Training children in right habits strengthens their wills. Maturity is making right choices. We want our children to have strong wills for doing what is right — strong wills for doing God's will. Crushing the will is not training the will. Training requires a relationship between parent and child. It requires patience and persistence on the part of both parent and child. When you train a child, you both grow in virtue.

I am not asserting that corporal punishment is wrong. I am asserting that it should not be necessary. Charlotte Mason writes of this eloquently:

> *Discipline does not mean a birch-rod, nor a corner, nor a slipper, nor a bed, nor any such last resort of the feeble. The sooner we cease to believe in merely penal suffering as part of the divine plan, the sooner will a spasmodic resort to the birch-rod die out in families. We do not say the rod is never useful; we do say it should never be necessary...Discipline is not punishment — What is discipline? Look at the word; there is no hint of punishment in it. A disciple is a follower, and discipline is the state of the follower, the learner, imitator...are by the very order of Nature, their disciples...He who would draw disciples does not trust to force; but to these three things to the attraction of his doctrine, to the persuasion of his presentation, to the enthusiasm of his disciples; so the parent has teachings of the perfect life which he knows how to present continually with winning force until the children are quickened with such zeal for virtue and holiness as carries them forward with leaps and bounds. (Parents and Children, 66)*

We don't want self-controlled children. We want children who hear and answer the Lord. We need to give children choices within limits, but we need to teach them how and why to choose right. We need to train their hearts and educate their minds. When they are fully informed of the consequences of their actions, we need to allow free will, just as our heavenly Father does.

In order to train the child's will in this manner, parents must lay down their lives for them. They must be willing to spend large amounts of time engaged with them. They must believe that children are educated by their intimacies and they must ensure that the child is intimate with what is good and noble and true. And when the child needs correction, the parent must educate in the truest sense of the word. She must teach. Our children are created in the image and likeness of God. If she looks at the child, sees Christ in his eyes, and disciplines accordingly, she will train her children well.

Children who are trained in such a way do not have their will subdued; instead they have it inspired by the Holy Spirit. They have an appetite for all that is best: great literature, classical music, great art. Incidentally, the philosophical point that my professors differed on so many years ago was this: Secular educators say children are incapable of abstract thought until they are teenagers. My advisor disagreed, and so do I. Charlotte Mason would say that they can't think abstractly because they are being fed a steady diet of twaddle. Their brains are weak and lazy because everything given to them for sustenance is predigested and watered down. Give them great literature and art and music, and inspire them to aspire to greatness.

Education Is a Life

I think it is when we begin to view home education as a lifestyle that we begin to truly be liberated from what many Catholic homeschoolers see as bondage. We see that education is an atmosphere. It is a discipline. Finally, it is a life. This is where a whole-books education will liberate the mother. In a living-books home, we don't "do" school. We have lesson time, to be sure. But we don't do school. We are not slaves to the three "S"s of education: syllabus, scope, and sequence. We live in a learning environment all the time. Learning doesn't stop when lessons end. Because children live in an atmosphere of great ideas and because they have the habits that enable them to learn, they are learning all the time. They are living a learning lifestyle. And that is what this is all about.

I am not Charlotte Mason. I do not play her in my home. She lived one hundred years ago. I live today. She was British. I am American. She had no children. I am expecting my seventh baby. She had no household to manage. I most certainly do. She was Anglican. I am Catholic. She disapproved of competitive sports. I spend several hours a week driving to and from soccer practice. She did not have to contend with television and Nintendo. Unfortunately, I do.

She also did not have the benefit of Karen Andreola, Penny Gardner, and my very favorite, Sally Clarkson. These are women who have studied Charlotte Mason's philosophies and applied them to the here and now. I have learned so much from them. None of these women has benefited from the writings of Edith Stein. The lifestyle of learning that I propose takes the best from Charlotte Mason and her modern followers, prayerfully considers the wisdom of Saint Teresa Benedicta, and incorporates the whisperings of the Holy Spirit to me and to you. No book is complete. You will not find a perfect "how to" manual because each family must write its own. Home education is unique to each home.

Edith Stein writes, "We sometimes forget that we shall please Him best, and get more from Him…when we use what we have by nature to the utmost at the same time that we look out for what is beyond nature in the confidence of faith and hope" (*Woman*, 4). I will take what I discern to be the best of home education's ideas and mix them up with my own thoughts and those of my modern-day mentors, and I encourage you to do the same.

I hope you are considering bringing a lifestyle of learning into your home. Doing so can be a life-changing experience for your home and family. It may appear daunting to effect such a change in your home, particularly if you have found comfort in the syllabus, but starting is simple, and as you begin to see that all the world is a learning experience, you will joyfully embrace your role as the facilitator of your child's education.

Have teatime with your children sometime this week. Even the manliest of boys can be enticed to the table with the right sweet treat. Play classical music while you do chores. Slow down the pace and allow time to talk, flip through books, or just be. Read aloud a living book while everyone enjoys hot cocoa or lemonade. Bring a

bunch of flowers into the house, put out a pretty tablecloth or look for other ways to bring in beauty. One day soon, bring out a coffee-table book on art (Monet, Rembrandt, Norman Rockwell are good choices) and choose a picture for everyone (yes, even the three-year-old!) to study and discuss. Change the background screen on your computer to a Mary Cassatt.

When doing studies, limit table time to ten or fifteen minutes per subject, but require complete attention. Begin to hone your own attention skills. Are you really listening when your child talks to you? If you are, then you can follow the rabbit trails of their interests and enthusiasm with living resources.

Consider letting your children help you plan. A child who is surrounded by living ideas will naturally find his curiosity piqued. When he takes some responsibility for planning, he becomes more invested in the learning. You will both be pleased with the results.

Help your children begin to record their experiences in a notebook, journaling what they have learned. Over time, their notebooks will grow fat and lend themselves to being divided, much the way a favorite plant grows well with loving care. Your children will be so proud of neat, carefully made notebooks that reflect their abundant education.

Go on a walk and really look; take your time; soak in His creation. Take along a backpack with whatever trail guides, magnifying glasses, and bug bottles you have, and plop down on a blanket somewhere and see what you can find and identify. Send the children out to find some "nature" and have them come back to report to you on it. Start a rock, leaf, bark, bug, butterfly, or stick collection. Take lots of zippered plastic bags.

 Take along some drawing pads or just plain paper and encourage your children to write or draw about what they see. This is the beginning of their nature journal. You start one, too.

Think about habits — which one would you identify to slowly start working on in each child — and in yourself? As you think about habits, ponder the words of Saint Thomas Aquinas: "Every power which may be variously directed to act, needs a habit whereby it is well disposed to its act … in the will we must admit the presence of a habit whereby it is well disposed to its act."

In order to bring this lifestyle of learning into your home, you must look for beauty and new ideas, listen to your children's interests and desires, create memories, look for new habits to develop, and give yourself and your children the grace of time to savor your time at home. Become involved with your children. Look at their hearts. Let them look at yours. Give them your focused attention. Edith Stein encourages, "The children in school do not need merely what we have but rather what we are" (*Woman*, 6).

Commit your learning home to prayer. What does He envision for you and your family? One thing is certain. He does not want your children to be educated by a woman who feels trapped and frantic. He does not want them to be guided by someone who is gritting her teeth to get through a dry, dusty curriculum with absolutely no kid-appeal, simply because that is what she has been told she must do. And he doesn't want you all to miss the wonder and splendor of the world He created for you because you are bound to the scope and sequence of a dated teacher's manual. Learning cannot, should not, be confined to the time our children spend at a table with a textbook. As their educator, your most important task is to change your mind-set so that you see the entire day and the entire week as an opportunity to learn. You cannot force these ideas into the old wineskins of school-based education.

The old wineskins are a system of education. They are an artificially contrived way of pouring facts into children. We seek to find a new method of education: a method whereby we instill in children a love of learning and then give them the tools to educate themselves.

Charlotte Mason writes about the difference between method and system:

> *We have a method of education, it is true, but method is no more than a way to an end, and is free, yielding, adaptive as Nature herself.*
>
> *Method has a few comprehensive laws according to which details shape themselves, as one naturally shapes one's behaviour to the acknowledged law that fire burns.*
>
> *System, on the contrary, has an infinity of rules and instructions as to what you are to do and how you are to do it. Method in education follows Nature humbly; stands aside and gives her fair play.*
>
> *A Method is not a System — System leads to Nature: assists, supplements, rushes in to undertake those very tasks which Nature has made her own since the world was.*
>
> *Does Nature endow every young thing, child or kitten, with a wonderful capacity for inventive play? Nay, but, says System, I can help here; I will invent games for the child and help his plays, and make more use of this power of his than unaided Nature knows how. So Dame System teaches the child to play, and he enjoys it; but, alas, there is no play in him, no initiative, when he is left to himself; and so on, all along the lines. System is fussy and zealous and produces enormous results — in the teacher!*
>
> (*Parents and Children*, 168–169)

Abandon the system. Adapt the method that is more natural for the child and for you. Don't be a slave to the syllabus. And let yourself be granted the freedom of home education.

In *Wisdom's Way of Learning*, Marilyn Howshall writes, "Ask God to enable you to see the old educational framework that underlies your hidden schooling assumptions. When the blind spots are exposed it is God who will empower you and transform the false ideas (a house built on sand) into truth (a house built on the Rock of Christ). This is the place where the Lord can show you how a Lifestyle for Learning can transform your home into one where learning is taking place at all times; a home where valuable activity is going on all day — not just during 'school time'. Not only is this the only way for [Christian] homeschooling to work, but this is also the only way to homeschool with joy, zeal and fun!"

Joy, zeal, and fun. Children come ready to embrace joy. If you are able to relinquish your old notions of education, you will allow the power of real-life education to be released in your life and your children's lives. Certainly, the traditional school's educational model was not something to emulate. There is so much more to life and to education than either the content or the process in any workbook.

Consider this note from *Wisdom's Way of Learning:* "Often, when we begin to 'homeschool,' as opposed to endeavoring to educate our children at home, we find security in bringing all that is school into our homes. We live according to that system so we can be like the world and have a 'real' school. But real school primarily emphasizes the outward appearance."

I call this the "mother-in-law trap." We want to look good to those who may be watching. We fall into the claws of pride and perfectionism as we try to adapt our new philosophy of wholehearted education to the old traditions of product-oriented education.

I remember being told by my second principal to be sure that I was doing all the same activities with my students as the other two first-grade teachers. She said, "The parents look at the papers at the end of the week. They talk and they compare. You will do fine as long as everything is the same."

The emphasis was entirely on product. No account was taken for the process of education. And — this is so, so important — no account was taken for the gifts and the calling of the child.

What does God want your child to do? What gifts has He blessed her with and how does He expect her to fully develop in order to serve Him? No two children in your household are the same. No two children will grow to love and serve the Lord in the same fashion. No two children should have the same education.

There is no prepackaged curriculum for the type of learning I am advocating. There is not even a list of what to cover each year. Miss Mason encouraged her teachers to present something new every quarter. She wanted them to keep challenging children with new ideas and to keep growing themselves. This plays beautifully into our goal of nurturing our children's vocations.

What delights him? What does he ask about? God put those delights on his heart. Now help him pursue them.

Does this sound hard? Does it sound like a lot of work? I assure you, this is the most liberating thing you can do for yourself as a home educator. Burnout happens when we try to meet someone else's goals, when we try to conform to someone else's style, and when we try to do with our children what was intended for someone else's child.

We need to know our purpose, to clearly identify our goal in education. From there, we need to focus upon our children. Really focus. Work on relationships. Concentrate on understanding the heart of the child. What makes him tick? What delights him? What are his struggles?

Last week, I went to the pond with another family. My children did not know the other children and, indeed, I didn't know the family well. The other mom and I thought the outing would be a success because we hold the same philosophy of education. And it was a huge success.

What I noticed was that our children did not pair off with each other according to age or gender but according to temperament. As I sat with the other mother and we compared notes on our children, we would look up and see similar children already playing together. This matched my seven-year-old with her three-year-old, a pair that would have seemed unlikely at first, but really surprised neither mother.

We knew the hearts of those children and we understood what drew them together. From there, we could introduce ideas that spoke to them. We were there, offering a word here and there and then stepping back to let them learn. We all enjoyed each other and we were all surprised to find that four hours had passed before we thought about turning for home.

To me, this is what home education is all about. It is educating the heart of a child within a family. It is not being confined in the basement or dining room of a house, plodding through a workbook. It is living together and learning about each other and challenging one another to greater heights. We don't keep them at home because we are afraid of the world. We don't keep them at home because we want to confine them to the dining-room table. We keep them at home to nurture them, to cultivate relationships with them, and to plant the seeds of relationships with other people and their ideas. We keep them at home to equip them to embrace and to shape the world of their Creator.

MacBeth Derham writes:

> At home, they can see what real life is about. They are surrounded by loved ones. They are encouraged. They are disciplined with love. I can keep out the bad, the twaddle, the insipid. I can bring in the good, the beautiful, the holy. Their love of learning is encouraged and nurtured and nourished. My favorite quote comes from Willa Ryan, another mother who has embraced this style of learning: "That's why I am homeschooling. Because I want our family to meet in heaven someday, and I think we have a better shot at it if we journey together as much as possible." I think this is where so many parents lose their children on the way. They let them go on the journey by themselves way too early. If we were traveling to Europe, would we let our three-year-olds go with a group of other three-year-olds? What about our four-year-olds? Seven-year-olds? Twelve-year-olds? The road to heaven is longer. Yes! Let's journey together!

We keep them at home so that we can journey together toward the ultimate destination. There is so much to point out along the way. We are not going to get far if we are chained to a desk, following someone else's educational plan.

Freedom is following God's plan for your family. Jesus said, "My yoke is easy and my burden is light" (Matthew 11:30). If educating your children at home is hard, if you feel heavily burdened, then you have not taken up His yoke. You need to discern what He wants for your family. And you need to pursue it with all your time and energy.

When all the world becomes your classroom, you are not bound to the table and the assignments for this week's syllabus. When you are prayerfully discerning how to meet the individual needs of your child, and when you are open to the answers, life becomes simpler.

For instance, I mentioned that I spend a good bit of time driving my children to soccer practice. Without bias, I can say that my children are exceptional athletes. I don't know how God will use that in their lives, but I do feel called to nurture their talents. We spend hours in the car. During that time we have built a house at Pooh Corner, we have felt our tummies rumble at the description of goodies prepared by Dickon's mother and shared in the Secret Garden. We have flown to Neverland with Wendy, Michael, and John. We have skated with Hans Brinker and climbed in the Alps with Heidi. We have shivered in Narnia and in the attic of the Little Princess.

When we arrive at our destination, my eldest tumbles out of the car to kick the ball around for two hours and the rest of us take a walk around the lake. We carry our nature backpacks, which are always packed and ready in the back of the car. My budding naturalist, who cannot sit still inside for more than ten minutes, is delighted to be in the great outdoors, and so is his two-year-old sister, the intrepid bug catcher.

My children don't consider their time in the car, on the soccer field, or around the lake to be "school." They consider it to be life. It is my life too. The happy coincidence is that we are all learning great lessons from this life that we share.

Don't be afraid to use a resource that isn't stamped "Catholic." Be discerning, but not afraid. When you discern what is best to feed your child's mind, consider this: Charlotte Mason wrote, "Nourish a child daily with loving, right, and noble ideas...which may bear fruit in his life." (*Parents and Children*, 228–229) Kimberly Hahn and Mary Hasson echo that thought: "Authentic Catholic education relies on and includes all that is true, good, and beautiful — in short, everything that points the way to God, the source of all truth, goodness, and beauty. Yet not every curriculum source that meets this criterion comes wrapped in paper stamped 'Catholic.' And, sadly, not everything that proclaims itself 'Catholic' truly is." (*Catholic Education: Homeward Bound*, 163–164)

As you plan for your child's educational experiences, won't you please be certain that you are nourishing him well and educating him with and for Life? Take to heart and to prayer the words of Edith Stein: "... the small, small child with its physical-psychic disposition and its innate singleness of purpose is delivered into the hands of human sculptors. The fulfillment of his goal depends on whether or not they furnish the necessary formative materials for his body and soul." (*Woman*, 131)

Words from the Wise

Isn't placing Saint Teresa Benedicta next to Charlotte Mason and trying to integrate the two just an attempt to Catholicize the Charlotte Mason philosophy of education? After all, Charlotte Mason was Protestant; how can we look to her for guidance as we plan an authentic Catholic education?

MacBeth Derham, New York

The Charlotte Mason/Edith Stein "relation" is the result of thinking in a Charlotte Mason kind of way. Charlotte Mason's philosophy is often of the traditional "liberal-arts" kind in content. As parents, we seek to help our children become lifelong learners. As Catholics, we look for ways to give our children a classical liberal arts education. A Charlotte Mason education can provide for these criteria. But where has the real liberal-arts education in Catholic schools gone?

The trend toward text/workbooks, and the trend away from primary sources and real experiments, the trend away from time to evaluate what we have learned ("free time for thinking"), replaced by hours of homework, the trend toward anthologizing our literature, and the trend toward twaddle, have all removed Catholic education, even in the homeschool, from the glorious realm of the liberal arts. Charlotte Mason's methods can restore this heritage to home education.

Willa Ryan, California

Well, also it is a Catholic way. Catholics take and sanctify or baptize the good in things, and discard what is not good or wholesome. This is closer to the Biblical model where Saint Paul says "everything is good ...not everything is beneficial," and where Saint Peter changed the Christian disciplines to allowing the eating of meat sacrificed to idols, and making circumcision optional.

So I think it sort of ironic to criticize for "Catholicizing" Charlotte Mason since this has such a noble Catholic tradition — e.g. Saint Paul speaking on Mars Hill and talking about the unknown God.

I've looked and looked through Charlotte Mason's books. I've found some things that are emphasized differently than a Catholic might, but I've never found anything inherently contradictory to Catholic orthodoxy. Even if there were, that would not mean that all the good things need to be discarded. Many of Charlotte Mason's principles are beneficial in living the Catholic lifestyle.

Having converted and found the fullness of the faith, I do hate to see Catholics acting like the dwarves in Narnia, huddling next to the door and thinking they are still in a dark and stuffy stable.

The Art of Language Arts

~ Teaching Reading ~

Nowhere is the benefit of a real-life, real-books education more evident than in the teaching of reading. Although I did not set out to read to my children in utero, that is exactly what happened. My first child listened, all tucked up tight, while I read to the first graders in my classroom. All of his siblings have listened to our family reading times. After they are born, the reading continues — hours of it a day — before naps, at bedtime, and at "cranky time." We love to share books together. The best way to describe how to teach reading begins with the smallest child. Learning to read is a journey that begins when children are very young.

Reading is a developmental process. In many ways, reading and writing are analogous to listening and speaking. Just as you are your child's first and best teacher of spoken language, so too are you the best teacher of written language. Teaching reading is not a science. It is an art which requires loving patience. Like so much of parenting, there is no one right way to do it. Like so many learning processes, not all children develop reading skills at the same pace.

Unfortunately, reading is often the first litmus test of home education's success. "Can he read?" is one of the inevitable questions asked by anxious skeptics. Grant Colfax, son of the authors of *Homeschooling for Excellence*, did not read until he was nine; he went on to be a Harvard graduate and Fulbright scholar. Early readers are not necessarily better readers or better students. Just because a child takes more time to develop a skill does not mean he will be less proficient.

It is crucial to lay a solid prereading foundation and to instill in a child a love of a good story and a respect for the world of knowledge that reading holds. Take care not to shortchange the prereading stage in your rush to "teach" reading.

Good reading instruction begins first with good literature and an understanding of what print is. The child needs to understand the spoken word, which can be written down and read both silently and aloud. Then we can move on to include solid phonics instruction in order to equip the child with a firm foundation in word attack skills. Many prereading activities are things you have done since your child was very little, while some are more formal. All can and should be adapted as the child grows older and his reading ability improves.

Your first objective is to develop a sense of story. Help the child to understand that a story has a beginning, middle, and end — that it imparts meaning. Read or tell stories using the Directed Listening-Thinking Activity, educator's terminology for asking a child to predict what will happen based on title and pictures and what he already knows about the subject, and stopping periodically throughout reading to confirm or change predictions and discuss the story. The best method for this is the one you've been using all along. Cuddle up in bed or sit the child on your lap.

Never feel guilty about taking "real" school time to read aloud. This time has great value in home education. Reading aloud to a child is a means of introducing him to all the facets of good literature: fine vocabulary, excellent syntax, compelling stories, and beautiful illustrations. It increases a child's vocabulary and encourages oral language growth by exposing a child to rich language unavailable elsewhere. It encourages the development of the habit of attention in listening.

While my family certainly frequents the library, we also have an extensive collection of books at home. These are books I read over and over again. As a hidden benefit, these books become old friends, familiar in story and language, and they are the perfect springboards into fluent reading.

By discussing the story as you read, you are encouraging the child to read for comprehension. You are focusing on reading as a thinking process, not merely a word-calling product. This distinction is of the utmost importance. You want the child to be engaged. You are encouraging him to think, involving him in the text, piquing curiosity, improving memory, encouraging divergent thinking, and maintaining his attention. Reading aloud is particularly suited to the home education environment. Millions of dollars have been poured into creating big books for classrooms so that classroom teachers can re-create the lap method of reading. You can do this at home with the real thing on a real lap. It works very well with two or more siblings, and you can nurse the baby at the same time.

Choose quality literature with rich — not stilted — text and engaging illustrations. My favorite sources for choosing picture books are *The Read Aloud Handbook* by Jim Trelease, *Books Children Love* by Elizabeth Wilson, *Five in a Row* by Jane Claire Lambert, and *Peak With Books* by Marjorie R. Nelsen and Jan L. Nelsen. The activities suggested in the latter two resources are excellent examples of literature-based reading and writing instruction.

Pay particular attention to books that emphasize story structure. Children need to understand that a story goes somewhere. Good books for reinforcing story structure are predictable books, pattern stories, and circle stories. Circle stories are those that follow the home-adventure-home pattern like in *Peter Rabbit*, *The Story of Ping*, and *Where the Wild Things Are*. Follow up listening to such stories by drawing the event inside a circle using pie-shaped wedges, moving in a clockwise manner from home through the events of the adventure and back home again. Expand on the theme by using a circle to record a day trip from the child's own experience and then asking him to dictate the story using cues from the circle while you write it down. Illustrate it together and read it over and over.

Pattern stories are stories like *If You Give a Mouse a Cookie*, *Brown Bear, Brown Bear*, *Drummer Hoff*, and *I Know an Old Lady*. These are fun to read, and children will quickly memorize and pretend to reread. Sit a four-year-old down to "read" to a two-year-old. The two-year-old gets a story and the four-year-old has a huge sense of pride while reinforcing things like left to right progression, "book talk" vocabulary, and print to speech matching. Predictable books have a brief, repetitive text and foster the same experience as pattern books.

In addition to developing a sense of story, a child must develop a concept of *word*. The child needs to understand what a word is. You have known what a word is for so long that you probably don't give it a second thought. For a child, the concept of a unit of speech comprised by certain specific symbols, bounded by space to which a specific meaning is assigned, is a very advanced concept.

One of the best ways to develop a concept of word is to record the child's own speech in writing and read it back to him repeatedly, pointing out familiar words. This is called the Language Experience Approach to reading, and it is a highly effective way to teach both reading and writing when used in conjunction with literature and a solid phonics program.

For example, I encourage my young children to tell a story of their own or describe a trip. Sometimes a child will do this individually; other times two or three will collaborate. I write down the story, word for word, ignoring the natural urge to improve upon the child's language. Then the story is reread aloud to the child. Usually as I reread, I point to each word. He is given a chance to illustrate it.

With a four- or five-year-old who has begun to show an interest in the written word, I will use his own text and ask him to circle words he recognizes. Usually the first to be circled are names of friends and family members. A child who can recognize and recall the shape of a word is demonstrating a visual readiness for reading.

Developmental readiness to read cannot be hurried. Your child will be physically and mentally ready to read according to the plan of his Maker — not you and not the county. As your child begins to find certain words recurring in his own writing, and as he begins to recognize words in his environment — the brand name on the washer, the sign on the grocery bag that matches the sign on the store, the titles of favorite books — help him to make a word bank.

Print the words on 3 x 5 cards and put them in a special box you have chosen for this purpose. Read the cards in isolation frequently. No word should be in the box unless it is a sight word. An important component to fluency is instant recognition of highly frequent words. These are sight words, and you should endeavor to teach them to an early reader so that the child will not get "stuck" sounding them out over and over again (especially since many of them are irregular). Begin to make a collection of words that pop up frequently in your child's reading and writing and play games with these words written on index cards. This bank will be the foundation that propels him into phonics. In addition to his own stories, word-bank words can come from rhymes, stories, and songs that have been read to him.

Using his word bank, have your young reader find words that could be used to describe a certain object. Encourage him to illustrate the noun cards. A child can alphabetize the word-bank words to the first letter; provide dividers for the boxes. Once the words are alphabetized, help him make a personal dictionary using magazine pictures to illustrate the meaning of word-bank nouns. Play Go Fish or Bingo with the words. Make duplicate cards and play Concentration. Use movable letters to let the child try to spell the words in his bank.

When a child has a working knowledge of about fifty sight words, begin to teach phonics patterns. Children need to recognize that a vowel, by itself, does not have a regular sound. Vowels are affected by the letters around them. But vowel patterns are highly regular. These patterns, called *rimes* by linguists, are the key to fluent reading. Fluent readers do not sound out a letter at a time. Instead, they recognize the rimes and they combine them with the consonants that precede them. In multisyllabic words, they learn to divide the word according to rimes, to decode the rimes, and then to combine them.

During shared reading time, choose a word that has a regular phonics pattern and is likely to have several words which rhyme with it. Ask your child to help make a list of rhyming words. Let him practice writing the rime and then point out the various consonants and consonant blends that precede the rime in each word. Practice reading the list frequently over a few days until you are satisfied that the child knows all the words. Then choose a new pattern to repeat the process. Make the lists readily available to the child when he is writing his own stories and remind him of the pattern when he meets a word he doesn't recognize but which has the rime in it. Teach the child to look at the rime as a unit and to decode in units. Books of nursery rhymes, Dr. Seuss books, and illustrated picture books of poetry (like Susan Jeffers' version of *Stopping by Woods on a Snowy Evening*) are good springboards for this activity.

Once a beginning reader has mastered the words in a word family, add those words to the word-bank box. After he has several families in the box, play word sort games with your learner. Initially, sort by beginning consonant sounds, eventually moving on to middle and final sounds. Then sort by vowel patterns. Don't isolate individual vowel sounds; instead, look at the pattern. This activity, combined with teaching consonant sounds and consonant blends, is the single most effective phonics lesson you give.

It is possible to teach reading, with a firm phonics foundation, with no phonics text at all. Focus on word families and word-bank activities and lots of reading of the child's own dictated writing. Provide lots of practice from those books you have read over and over since he was little. In this supportive environment, providing the child is ready, he will read. While it is not a textbook, Patricia Cunningham fully develops this idea in her book *Phonics They Use: A Guide for Classroom Teachers*. I highly recommend it.

If you must use a packaged phonics curriculum to feel confident teaching beginning readers, I recommend *Alphaphonics*. With that book, concentrate on helping the child to see predictable patterns in words. Don't focus on singular letter sounds. Limit lessons to ten minutes at a time and concentrate more time on reading aloud to the child. Teach the child to employ the strategies of word family decoding in the world of real books.

What if letter patterns just don't click with your child? Stop. Change direction. Emphasize listening skills, vocabulary development and reading aloud. Read lots and lots of rhyming books. Memorize nursery rhymes and then point to the words. Use lots of variety and lots of practice at this stage. Cut letters and words from ads, use chalk and markers, a pan of rice to write in, a paintbrush and water on the sidewalk, pudding to finger-paint, and magnetic letters. With time, the child will recognize whole words and not need to sound them out every time. Remember, it is also okay to teach a whole word. In the beginning, children will get bogged down and frustrated if you try to teach a phonics rule with every word. Concentrate on patterns and not on rules. Spelling is easier too when the child understands the patterns.

Try not to think of phonics and "whole language instruction" (reading in the context of a real story) as a dichotomy. The key is balance. When the schools switched to whole language, they claimed that they did so because reading instruction based solely on phonics was not producing the type of readers they wanted. They wanted thinking readers with strong comprehension skills, not readers who were merely word callers. They wanted children who interact with the text and pictures as they read. And they wanted children to love reading because the stories were so wonderful.

If those were the goals, they are worthy goals. Children who love reading will be excellent readers. The problem is that many schools threw out the baby with bath water and didn't give the children the skills needed to decode the text. Children need both phonics and great literature. They need the balance of meaningful stories and decoding skills. The schools are turning back to phonics and have been thrown into a very costly state of utter confusion. They also have eight to ten years' worth of children who are very poor readers taught solely with the whole language, look-say approach.

As home educators, we can take the best of both worlds and create the ideal reading curriculum for our children. Maintain a balanced approach to reading instruction. Spend a short period each day on phonics and never sacrifice real reading time for rules instruction. A child who is taught phonics in the context of a literature-based program will rapidly develop into a fluent reader.

Once your child begins to acquire basic reading skills don't kill the desire to read with too much drill and practice. Get him reading high-interest books or magazines. I give my children phonics instruction for ten to fifteen minutes a day until they are able to read easy readers fluently. Then I back off and let the child teach himself the rest. I

wait to start phonics instruction until the child shows an interest in reading (a lesson I learned the hard way). I drop it as soon as the child indicates that he is confident enough to read something about which he cares.

My first child wanted to be able to read *Sports Illustrated for Kids*. Because he was highly motivated to decode that text and *because he brought a great deal of personal knowledge and interest to the text*, he really taught himself to read after a solid phonics introduction. It is also infinitely helpful, when a child is on the verge of fluency, to revisit all those old favorites he has heard again and again. It is perfectly acceptable and even desirable to encourage fluency with high-interest, easily attainable texts.

My second child proceeded in much the same way as the first. He was determined to read *The Beginner's Bible* by himself. He had heard the stories repeatedly for years. Many of them he had memorized word for word. With confidence, he met words like "Bethlehem" and "Philistines" without more than a moment's hesitation. He matched the printed word to what he knew and then he knew the word. Recognition was rapid and fluency followed. He never did a single phonics worksheet. He never read a basal reader designed and contrived to teach phonics. My goal was not to have him complete reams of phonics worksheets nor was it to stumble through basal readers that did not inspire or hold his interest. My goal was for him to read as naturally as he breathes — for him to want to "own" everything in print. My goal was to have him blossom into a thinking reader who automatically reads the backs of cereal boxes just because they are there.

Teaching Writing

The beauty of an education that relies upon living books to impart knowledge is…living books. Good literature is inspiring. One of our overarching goals in a home-education environment is literacy. We want proficient, effective readers and writers. We want children who care enough about what they are reading that they ask questions. We want children who know how to find information. And we want them to know how to communicate the answers to those questions. Our children are in the process of becoming literate, and the environment in our homes is designed to support the process.

A living-books education is an integrated approach to teaching writing. We begin with a story — a well-written story. The story drives the learning. In order for the method to be effective, a child must interact with the text. For a young child, this interaction takes place when he is comfortably seated on Mom's lap, helping to turn pages and asking questions or making comments as she reads. The book engages them both. C.S. Lewis once noted that a good children's book appeals to and inspires adults as well. On this note, don't limit your use of quality picture books to your youngest children only. There is much of value for an older child as well. In addition to relevant content, an older child can learn storytelling techniques, rich vocabulary, and many art techniques. These books also provide dramatic reading practice to emerging and fluent readers.

In our home, storybooks are the springboards to numerous activities. Sometimes, we are inspired to make a book of our own, modeled after one we have read. For instance, after reading *If You Give a Mouse a Cookie*, my children wrote and illustrated "If You Give a Horse Some Breakfast Cereal." In the process, they learned a great deal about repetitive story structure. When children model their own stories after stories they have read, they begin to integrate story structure into their knowledge base and apply it to the writing process.

Plan to devote at least a half hour every day to writing. For young children, "writing" is actually dictation. You enable the child to write by separating composition from handwriting. While a child certainly needs to learn handwriting, he doesn't need to be frustrated by it when he is trying to convey something meaningful. Remember the Language Experience Approach? It is writing instruction as well as reading instruction.

Enable your child to understand that the printed word is speech written down by writing his own speech for him. Young children, particularly boys, struggle with handwriting. It is slow and laborious. But they have so much to say. Encourage them to say it — then write it down or keyboard it for them.

Suggest that a child keep a prayer journal. Let him choose a book that is beautifully bound. Here, he can write and draw what is important to him. It is okay to use invented spelling in such a journal because the Lord can read it — He knows what is on your child's heart. There are plenty of other opportunities for you to gently correct spelling. Here, it is ideas on paper that are important.

As your child approaches adolescence, you might consider a dialogue journal. Begin the dialogue yourself. Write him a letter, telling him why he is important in your life. Explain that you want to use the journal as a means of communication between the two of you. Perhaps look over a baby book together and then explain that you want him to help chronicle the memories of his teenage years. This book will be precious indeed.

Instead of book reports, try character diaries. For each book they read, have children pretend they are a character in the book. They write diary entries as those characters would have. This exercise requires that the child interact with the text and reflect upon it, making both content and quality his own.

Don't overlook letter writing as an important vehicle for teaching good communication skills. Encourage pen pals, writing for information, writing to newspaper editors, and writing thank-you notes. Children love e-mail. When my husband worked in an office, my children took turns sending him a "lunchtime update" every day.

The cornerstone of a real-life, real-books education is *narration*. When a child is read a story or reads it himself, he is required to retell it, with as much detail as possible, after paying close attention to the first and only reading. After a trip to an historical site or a day in an apple orchard, the same method is employed, encouraging the child to use rich, descriptive language to tell about what he knows and cares about. Young children narrate orally, with Mom occasionally transcribing what is said. Some young children will naturally use drawings to express themselves, and these, too are narrations, either with or without captions. Older children, at around ten years old, begin to write their narrations.

The benefits to this approach are numerous. Because they are required to narrate after hearing a story or passage read only once, children learn quickly to pay close attention to that reading. They also learn to pay the same attention to the many facets of a field trip. The more details they notice, the more detailed their narrations. Children as young as four can be trained to be very observant and to retell stories and events with amazingly complex, textured language and sentence structure. It is the ideas in the stories or the experiences that fuel the narrations. These products, child-produced oral histories or essays, are a far cry from fill-in-the blank workbook pages or the questions at the end of a textbook chapter.

Narrations require that the child engage his heart. He must be personally connected with the idea being presented in order to recount it. He will also interact with the story as he retells it, infusing it with his own character. For instance, the Gospels are narrations and the charism of each apostle is evident when one compares each retelling of the same event.

Charlotte Mason writes, "A single reading is a condition insisted upon because a naturally desultory habit of mind leads us all to put off the effort of attention as long as a second or third chance of with our subject is to be hoped for. It is, however, a mistake to speak of the 'effort of attention.' Complete and entire attention is a natural function which requires no effort and causes no fatigue…the concentration at which most teachers aim is an innate provision for education that is not the result of training or effort." (*A Philosophy of Education, 171*)

In a household where narration is a daily habit, children learn to listen carefully the first time. They learn to pay close attention while reading (an art that is all but lost in an age of readily available information). They also learn to express themselves effectively. It is this expression that will be the hallmark of an excellent education. A child's ability to communicate well, both verbally and on paper, is absolutely essential.

It does not matter what he knows unless he can convey that knowledge well. The most important thing our children can do, and indeed the call of each and every child, is to go out and make believers of every nation. They cannot do that unless they can tell the Good News clearly and compellingly.

Narration can take on many forms. The most effective narrations in our household are dinnertime talks. Simply, my husband asks the children what they learned that day. Instead of replying, "About plants," they must tell him everything they learned about plants that day. Because I try to do as much family-style teaching as possible — that is, they are all learning about the same topic — each child contributes to the conversation. The children must make some of the knowledge "their own" in order to be able to tell about it later. Incidentally, these talks keep me on my toes too, I am certain to make sure that my children all learn something everyday in order to be able to tell about it at dinnertime.

This kind of narration — simple, informal retelling — is all that is necessary until about age five. Then, I generally record their retellings and encourage the children to illustrate them. I gather all narrations pertaining to a certain topic behind a subject divider in a three-ring notebook. When the section grows fat enough, it becomes a book. My kindergartners usually have a book of Bible stories, a book of fairy tales, and a nature notebook. They also have a book of field-trip narrations and souvenirs.

These books are excellent sources of material for Language Experience Approach reading practice for emerging readers. Because they are written in the child's own language, a beginning reader has a wealth of context support. The challenge is Mom's: do not overedit. Remember to preserve the integrity of the child's language so that he can begin to understand that the printed word is simply speech written down.

A ten-year-old is usually ready to begin to write his own narrations. Some children will be chomping at the bit to write and others will need to be encouraged. Take some time with the transition. At first, the written narrations will be much shorter than the dictated ones. It is important to keep taking dictation at this stage so that all the progress made in developing depth and detail isn't lost because the child is encumbered by the mechanics of writing.

Narration requires a child to interact with the knowledge in order to tell about it. Because each child brings different strengths and weaknesses to the process, we must acknowledge that not every child will always read and then write about what he has read. First, this would quickly get boring: read and write; read and write. Secondly, it would fail to tap into the burgeoning talents of a child. I have a child for whom at least one narration a week is a political cartoon from the historical period we are studying. This child has a gift for drawing and a very sophisticated, dry sense of humor. He must understand the subject matter in order to reflect upon it in a cartoon. My purpose of checking for understanding is fulfilled and his talents and interests are nurtured.

Not all his narrations can be drawings though, because he must learn to write well. Here, as in all of education, we strive for balance. My second child dislikes drawing and, frankly, has less aptitude for it. I consider drawing an essential component of education, so we offer him some instruction and require that he work toward some proficiency. Then we are sure to provide another venue for narrations — one which he enjoys. This child loves the computer. He is overjoyed with the opportunity to dictate while I keyboard his adventures or stories to be e-mailed to his godparents or his cousins. These too, can be printed and saved in a notebook. The record keeping takes care of itself.

In our home, narrations are enhanced by drawings, photographs, maps, tour brochures, and ticket stubs. Clear plastic page protectors hold a wonderful assortment of memories. In nature notebooks, pressed flowers, wheat from Mount Vernon, or watercolor paintings are kept safe inside page protectors. I encourage the children to label everything with the date and place. We have all learned how quickly we forget. We also take photographs of everything. The children help me lay out pages of photos with captions. Once again, they are narrating.

I have just begun video narrations. It seems I never think to grab the video camera when we are in the midst of something. My children are growing and changing so quickly and I want to preserve their speech and mannerisms. I also want them to see how they have grown. Every couple of weeks, I sit them down and let them tell the camera what they are learning and doing. They love to see themselves on camera and even the shyest child will talk for much longer than he would if I weren't behind a lens. I am using one tape per child. At the end of the year, we will have quite a treasury of oral narrations!

A child's own reading and writing become the source of reading, grammar, and spelling instruction. When a child is dictating stories, simply point out capital letters and punctuation as the story is keyboarded or when you read the stories together. Over time, the rules of writing become very familiar.

For a child who is writing his own narrations, editing is necessary. I choose one essay a week to edit. I keyboard it, with all errors. Together, we run the grammar check and spell check programs on the computer. The computer becomes the objective "bad guy." I am simply the supportive mentor who explains it all. Of course, this method is not foolproof; the computer will not pick up every mistake and it will indicate mistakes where there are none. It is a good beginning, however.

A season of grammar is necessary. There are several programs available to home educators that will get the job done. I don't think it is necessary to struggle through a grammar book year after year.

As a child becomes comfortable writing, he should be exposed to different sorts of writing in his reading and encouraged to copy those styles. Narrations can be poems, newspaper articles, personal experiences, historical fiction, even plays. A child who is studying the best examples of this writing in a real and relevant context will learn how to write from the very best writers.

Copy work and dictation have their place here. For small children, copy work is handwriting practice: First a letter, then a word, then a phrase, then a verse. All are done to the very best of the child's ability and saved in the notebook. Excellence is expected.

As a child matures, copy work is the careful study of literature. It is a child's chance to become familiar with the text of great writers, word by word and phrase by phrase. A child copies the work and in doing so learns the intricacies of it on an intimate level. In our house, we study a style of writing or a particular author every six weeks.

Dictation is the opportunity for a child to incorporate all he has learned of grammar and spelling. Of dictation, Laura Berquist writes, "Studied dictation is a useful tool in the development of children's writing ability. First, the children are working from models of good writing. They see and study correct usage, punctuation, and spelling, as well as excellent writing of various styles. In the old days of Catholic education, schools were financially poorer, but they turned out excellent scholars, as well as faithful Catholics. One reason for this was that neither the children nor the schools could afford books, so lessons were copied and then worked on. This meant that the children were continuously exposed to models of correctly written material. This is another example of the truth that children learn by imitation." (*The Harp and the Laurel Wreath*, 14–15)

For the very young child, I simply dictate words and sentences from the phonics patterns and storybooks we are currently studying. Our phonics lessons are extracted from rhyming books primarily. As the student becomes a capable reader, dictation passages are taken from copy work material. First we read and discuss the material, noting grammatical patterns or spelling of note. The next day, the child copies it (this may take two days). The third day, he studies it. Then I dictate to him as he writes it. The copy work and final dictation both go in his notebook.

The older child's spelling comes from his dictation work and his own writing. I pull misspelled words from his writing, write them correctly and have him copy them ten times. If I notice a pattern to his mistakes, I will have him copy several words that have the same pattern. There are so many theories on spelling, and I have to admit that I am not yet certain which one I believe. For right now, my approach is prescriptive/diagnostic: find the mistake, correct it, and teach any other words likely to present the same opportunity for a mistake.

The other day, a neighbor asked me to help her with her eight-year-old. His teacher asked him to write an essay for homework entitled "I Am a Pencil." An hour later, after much cajoling (hers) and whining (his), he was still staring at a blank piece of paper. This child didn't have the tools for writing. He hadn't seen the writing process modeled. He had a limited exposure to good writing examples (he was reading typical public school fare which is not exactly inspiring). And he didn't care about the topic. He was not a pencil, nor did he want to be one. The project was destined to fail.

Where do we begin to inspire a child to write and to equip him to write well? If he is not yet reading, it is easy. He will be offered ideas and experiences upon which he will reflect. He will be encouraged to narrate orally. He will listen to good literature and be given many varied opportunities to interact with text and pictures until he evolves into a fine reader and writer. If he has been a slave to another system, we liberate him. We support him. We read and write with him until he is ready to compose on his own. We provide the ideas and the tools and we get out of the way. He will learn to write, just as he learned to speak and we must approach the latter process with as much support, encouragement, and patience as we approached the former.

What follows is an example of a narration written by a six-year-old who has clearly been influenced by a wealth of fine literature read aloud to her. She dictated the following letter to her mother:

Nesting Tree
Fairwinds Lane
Virginia

March 12, 2002

My dear Cousin Merry,

How are you? It is I, your cousin Cherry Bluebird. I am fine. A family with three little girls moved into the house beside Nesting Tree, and I can look into their window and see what they are doing whenever I like! They have a baby one-year-old (I saw her birthday party), a six-year-old who this year will be seven, and a little three-year-old who likes to stand upon the window sill.

There are not many cars on the street.

I must tell you of the funny sight I saw on Friday. There were cows across the street in the neighbor's backyard! The inhabitants of the house scared away the cows. They were eating this and that as they walked slowly, with lumbering steps, up the hill I live on.

Builders are building a white house that's kind of like the house beside Nesting Tree.

Once I saw the baby of the house reach her head back and say, "Mwah!" Then she fell into her big six-year-old sister's arms, and her big sister put her on the Ikea table. (I have no idea where it came from. From Ikea, I suppose.)

It is nesting time. I will probably find a hole in a tree near here. I enclose a picture of me when this letter was finished. I have drawn green buds on Nesting Tree since St. Patrick's Day is coming — and the tree is budding.

Well, I must finish up this letter, for I cannot write much more. The leaves will soon open, and I must go and find my new home.

Love,
Cousin Cherry Bluebird

Narrated by Kate Peterson

As a child reads widely, he becomes a critic in his own right. Below is an example of literary criticism and narration, written by my son Michael when he was eleven:

My experience with Harry Potter was very decisive to say the least. It took me just one book to decide not to read the rest of the series. Eleven-year-old Harry Potter lives with the Dursleys, his aunt and uncle, and their spoiled son, Dudley. The Dursleys despise Harry for coming into their lives as an infant in a basket on their front porch. Mrs. Dursley's sister, Harry's mother, died alongside her husband. They were both wizards. The evil Lord Voldermort came to the Potter household when Harry was one to try to bring the Potters to the dark side. When the Potters refused, he killed the couple but Harry was too powerful for the lord and only was scarred.

The boy grows up thinking his parents died in a car accident. On Harry's birthday, a mysterious letter comes in the mail from a school that teaches boys and girls to become witches and wizards. On the day it's time to leave for the school, Hogwarts, the real adventure begins. Harry learns to make potions, how to transfigure rats into hairpins and other useful things.

The book consistently stumbles on the topic of right and wrong. For example: Harry and his classmates are learning how to fly on broomsticks when the teacher is called away for awhile. She tells the students to stay put and not to fly! Well, the school bully, Draco Malfoy decides to pick on one of the students by picking up the boy's broomstick and flying off. Harry Potter flies after Malfoy and just as Harry zooms up, the culprit goes down. The teacher catches Harry up in the air and she pretends to scold him in front of the class but then commends him for his flying ability behind closed doors. These kinds of mixed-message incidents happen throughout the book.

The book takes a very sinister, troublesome spin when Harry comes face to face with Voldermort. When the dark lord failed to kill Harry, he lost all his power. So he looks over the world trying to find someone to possess. With the body of a man in his control, Voldermort attacks Harry. The boy is so strong Voldermort's hands blister and burn when he touches Potter. The power is so great the body perishes but the dark lord filters into the air to find another victim.

The book's satanic references were very disturbing as can be imagined. I don't think it's appropriate for little children. The author also portrays the muggles (non magic folk) to be idiotic bumblers that have no clue about anything. The children in this book as well as the adults are very disrespectful. There is a lot of lying and cheating by both adults and children that goes unpunished. Many controversial things in the text were not needed, and they did not add any glory to this book. It was very disappointing.

A friend of my mom's told me that in the second book, Harry and his friends bury a screaming mandrake root. The more the root screams, the more dirt they dump on it. A mandrake root looks like a baby. In case the reader didn't know that, there is a picture of it at the beginning of the chapter. I wonder why the author picked a root that looks like a baby to bury. The author says that in the fourth book Harry's hormones are supposed to kick in. I don't even want to know what that's supposed to mean.

Instead of Harry Potter, I recommend the Redwall series of books by English author, Brian Jacques. The books are about abbey mice who live around the medieval time. The mice live in a great sandstone abbey. The hero of the books is Martin the warrior (a mouse featured in all the books). Martin defends Redwall Abbey from villainous ferrets, weasels, stoats, foxes, and rats. The warrior mouse appears alive in four books, and comes to new champions of Redwall as a guide in dreams (much like Obi-Wan Kenobi in the Star Wars films). The book has a very distinctive feeling of good and evil. The good abbey mice and their colleagues, portrayed by otters, moles, hares, hedgehogs, badgers, and squirrels, are exposed to many evils but always persevere through it all, never once dropping to evil's level. The books usually have very fierce battles that are described very graphically. The battles are very gory, and always the mice try to stop bloodshed from happening but once they are threatened to the point where combat is the only option, they fight. Always, mind you, the mice learn from the experience of war. The mice lose many friends and family during the wars but at the end of the book they always start to rebuild. The books have very rich literary style and are very entertaining for children and adults. The language really improves your grammar immensely.

Math cannot be confined to a written page.
It needs to be touched. Your child should play with it,
experiment with it, internalize it.
He should encounter the "Aha!" over and over again
during the years he learns at home.

Math with Meaning

It is often said that one of the unforeseen benefits of home education is that the teaching parent learns with her children. For me, this has been especially true in the discipline of mathematics. I had a terrible math education. My father was a naval officer, and we moved frequently during my elementary days. I missed core concepts along the way. I also was told very early that I "didn't have a head for math." I believed *that* until Patrick, my four-year-old, opened a whole new world for me.

With my first child, I used a wide array of materials and a solid text to teach math. I taught each lesson as it was intended, never resorting to ripping out the page and "just getting it done." As he approached the middle of second-grade math, I found myself with a baby and a toddler confusing my day. My eldest was reading by this time and did not need me to tell him what was expected on the math page. I left him to complete each page on his own, instructing him to come to me if he had a problem. This was the kiss of death. He learned to do the problems. He did them accurately. And he hated math. There was no meaning in it and no joy. Over time, his understanding began to slip, too. By the time baby Patrick was four, his big brother was struggling, and I needed a new outlook on math.

Patrick probably counted his own fingers and toes before I even had a chance to do so. He loves numbers and is fascinated by the delightful patterns that jump out at him all over this grand world. He has been blessed with being very mathematically inclined and being very verbal. This blessing has been a great gift to me. I am privileged to hear Patrick think aloud and to understand, at long last, the "Aha!" that is mathematics. Through his eyes, I see a predictable, regular science of precision that is so complex and yet so simple that it could only have been created by the Lord of the universe. I also see the challenge not to kill the natural love he has for math.

There are six children in my family now. We are all learning to love math together. It is a lesson that is more difficult for us older students. Just as I strive to create an environment rich in living literature, I strive to create and enjoy an environment that supports and encourages a mathematical way of thinking.

I find it curious that there is no mention of math in some Charlotte Mason "how-to" books and only passing mention in others. Miss Mason didn't seem terribly fond of math. Could it be that those of us who are drawn toward a literature-based curriculum are content to just get through what is required in math so that we can move on to "the good stuff," caught between the pages of living books? Can a math book be a living book?

Most importantly, can we expose our children to great ideas and great thinkers in this discipline and make math come alive for them? Our goal in mathematics education, just as in all education, is to provide for the child the opportunity to forge relationships and understand the discipline. When we start with a great story or a walk on the seashore or a beautiful painting, that goal seems attainable. Math too, can be a living discipline.

When a child is very young, begin to treat him to number games. Use a hundreds board to play with beans or color tiles and mark patterns. Teach skip counting (later called "multiplication") to a three-year-old by letting him place a tile on every third square; then chant the numbers of those covered squares. Play clapping, snapping, and patting pattern games; match dominoes; play store with money; use a spinner and count the squares of a classic Chutes and Ladders game. Tally a score.

The next time you have to wait at the doctor's office, let your young child play with the calculator. Without any guidance at all, he will find all sorts of interesting things it can do. When he tires of that, try math puzzles geared to children his age. Your child will enjoy the process and you may discover that math is much more fun that you remember it being.

The ability to grasp mathematical concepts is a developmental one. Watch your child for clues that he is ready to be introduced to typical elementary math concepts. Before a child can count (not rote recitation of numbers in order, but actual counting), he must understand that one corresponds to one. Given an equal number of trucks and plastic people, he should be able to put one person in each truck. When asked to set the table, he should have given one fork, one plate and one napkin to each person. He should be able to place one color tile on each square of a hundreds chart. He should have plenty of practice tallying, pointing, and counting items in a collection.

A child in this stage of development will love to work with attribute blocks and pattern blocks, sorting them according to color, size, or shape. Over time, he will understand the concept of a set, defined by specific characteristics. He will enjoy comparing and measuring, using nonstandard units like a length of string or a tower of Duplo blocks.

If you can, this is the time to invest in an assortment of math manipulatives. I feel a bit like a child in a candy store when I page through a manipulatives catalog. Admittedly, I also love the look of brightly colored "math toys" on the shelves of our learning room. I have made this investment over time, intending to use the manipulatives throughout the school years, not just in the early years.

Cuisenaire Rods are a basic learning tool that no home should lack. They were designed by a teacher named George Cuisenaire who applied his experience as a composer to come up with a "keyboard for mathematics." The rods are designed in graduated lengths beginning with a one-centimeter cube and ending with a ten-centimeter rod. Each length has a designated color, and children quickly learn which color has which value and how each color relates to another.

There are dozens of books available which use Cuisenaire Rods to teach almost any math concept. Indeed, an entire primary curriculum makes liberal use of them. Miquon math materials use simple, inexpensive workbooks and Cuisenaire rods to teach all concepts usually taught in the first through third grades.

The only thing Cuisenaire Rods don't do well is teach place value. For that, there is nothing like a set of base ten blocks. These include one-centimeter cubes similar to the unit cube in the Cuisenaire set, but they add tens rods, hundreds squares and thousands cube. Borrowing, carrying, and all those other concepts which tend to cause hair pulling will never be the same again!

Snap cubes or Unifix Cubes are ideal for teaching number concepts such as addition and subtraction. Snap cubes have an advantage over Unifix cubes, since they can be connected on all sides, bringing three-dimensional concepts into crystal clear focus.

Pattern blocks are an assortment of blocks of varied shapes and colors used for patterning, sorting, matching, one-to-one correspondence, similarity, and congruence. They also work well for teaching fractions. These blocks have proven useful over and over in my house, keeping a toddler purposefully engaged while I teach older children. Like all the manipulatives, they only come out at lesson time and they really make a very young child feel like part of the group.

Color tiles are also useful for exploring arithmetic and geometric ideas. They are exactly one inch and fit perfectly on a hundreds boards made of one-inch squares. Patterns on the hundreds board jump out in living color.

Attribute blocks are sets of blocks of varied shapes, colors, and thickness, which prove very useful for teaching the concept of sets. They are also used in the logic workbooks for very young children published by Critical Thinking Press.

None of these particular materials is necessary. A teaching mother can certainly make or find her own manipulatives. All of these, and the support manuals to go with them, will make her job much easier.

Commonly, teaching mothers search for the perfect math program. We think that if we decide on one publisher's text and workbook and we follow it faithfully, we won't have to give math another thought. Nothing could be further from the truth. Just like a text and workbook kill history or science, they kill math.

Math cannot be confined to a written page. It needs to be touched. Your child should play with it, experiment with it, internalize it. He should encounter the "Aha!" over and over again during the years he learns at home.

There is a school of thought that believes that children should discover math concepts on their own. There is another school of thought whose goal is that children simply learn the mechanics and memorize the facts. My children are in neither school. I do believe that children should have ample opportunity to "discover" concepts, but I do not think that they can construct an entire mathematical education on their own. It has taken the greatest minds centuries to construct the mathematical system we know today; my children are not going to discover it in my basement. I also believe they need to know how to solve a problem and to memorize facts. But that's not all they need.

Instead, I begin with a carefully crafted sequential list of concepts and introduce them using concrete objects. Such a list is readily available in each state's standard of learning objectives or in the scope and sequence of a good math textbook. I provide plenty of time and space to learn the concept using the manipulatives — masterly inactivity. Then I demonstrate how to represent the concept on paper. The children practice using standard symbols to represent mathematical ideas. The concept doesn't stop there. Most texts introduce with concrete objects and then leave those objects once the child is able to record on paper. We don't.

We revisit the concept again and again over time, using different manipulatives in order to solidify the concept. A child looks at the same concept differently as he matures. I bring much greater understanding to concepts I thought I mastered in the fourth grade now that I am more mature. We are unafraid to teach a child American history repeatedly in the first, fourth, and seventh grades, knowing he learns more each time. Math can be that way too. My fifth-grader's grasp of multiplication is better after playing multiplication math games with his younger brothers, even though he memorized all those facts when he was seven.

If we use a basic text as a guide, there is no reason to fear leaving out a critical component of a mathematical education. If we return again and again to the concrete manipulatives and the games, there is no reason to fear a "paper" knowledge of math that doesn't deepen and mature as the child grows. Just as the scientist begins with his fieldwork, consults his reference materials, and returns to his fieldwork over and over again, the mathematician returns again and again to his models, seeking to make sense of his expanding mathematical universe.

Drill has its place in a living math curriculum. Drill is necessary to provide the child with problem-solving tools. Plenty of drill develops speed and proficiency which ensures that the child won't be mired knee deep in a problem that is just beyond his reach. Because he has drilled basic facts, he can call upon them readily, using them as tools to solve meaty problems with real-life significance.

Drill can take several forms. Trusty timed drill sheets like Calculadders or those in the Saxon primary workbooks are invaluable for providing plenty of practice. Just be sure to avoid "drill and kill." One does not have to go with the other.

Math games are a true joy and accomplish the task of drilling painlessly. They also bridge age groups very well, a fact much appreciated by large families. Board games like Muggins!, Knock-Out, Equate, and Hive Alive: Bee Smart in Math" provide an opportunity for multiage play and very enjoyable drill. Be assured that they are not "bored" games. Game books like *Family Math* and *The I Hate Mathematics! Book* also have many multilevel teaching ideas.

There are living books for making math come alive for our children. Theoni Pappas has written several titles that fascinate children and make big concepts like pi"and Fibonacci sequences readily accessible. *Grandfather Tang's Story* by Ann Tampert is a lovely story, a beautiful art book, and a tangram book all in one. We need to build a math library as deliberately as we build a nature library, and we need to make time for math beyond the workbook.

We cannot shirk our responsibility to help our children learn to think like mathematicians. Ours is an increasingly complex, technological world. There is no ducking math — it's everywhere. Instead, we should encourage them to embrace the precision and the logic. We should provide the tools and present the living ideas. Children can be inspired by stories of mathematicians. They can be inspired to become mathematicians.

Elementary math essentially must teach children to compute and to solve problems. Computational skills include addition, subtraction, multiplication, and division. Children should learn both how and why to compute. Then they should memorize basic facts. Once the basics are mastered, they learn all over again using larger and smaller numbers. They learn place value, decimals, and fractions. In a real life-setting, they also learn about time, money, and measurement.

Have children construct tables, even if the process takes several days or weeks. Before memorizing addition or multiplication facts, they should work to complete tables, using concrete objects as necessary until they recognize the patterns.

Computation is the toolbox your child brings to problem solving. With real-life math problems and those in a book, the child must learn to discuss the problem, and you will be there to discuss it with him. He needs to know how to represent the problem symbolically on paper and to construct a visual or concrete model if necessary.

There is no perfect math text. I favor some programs more than others. The Saxon primary texts are wonderful for mothers who have never taught math before and need to be shown how to integrate manipulatives with concepts. There are even completely scripted lessons, perfect for mornings when one is struggling to teach despite having been up all night with a baby. After the third grade, Saxon changes abruptly. I am not a big fan of the texts that follow. They are stripped of the concrete and drill and kill mercilessly.

As previously noted, Miquon makes extensive use of Cuisenaire Rods. This program, when supplemented by Calculadders for extra drill, is a great core curriculum. It doesn't stand alone — it requires games and real-life experiences, but it is a good beginning.

In the middle years, I have struggled to find a good text that still incorporates concrete examples and varied practice. The *Key To...* series, supplemented by Calculadders and many, many manipulative activities, seems to work. This does require some planning and research on the part of the teaching parent. This is not a cookbook approach to math (though cooking is a great idea!). Instead, it is more a unit-study approach. The unit may be fractions or measurement or decimals. No matter what the topic, the teaching parent will utilize a variety of books, materials, and "experiments" to teach.

Once the solid foundation is laid, the Jacobs texts appeal to me most. Harold Jacobs' books are reviewed favorably by the upper elementary and high-schoolers I know who have used them. In itself, this is the sign of an engaging text. Children say that the books give them confidence previously missing in their approach to math. The text is not dry, but entertaining and, at times, even amusing.

Mathematics for Everyday Living is a series of workbooks geared toward older students which presents practical real-life applications of math in the context of careers which use those skills. For instance, *The Mathematics of Buying* covers unit prices, markups, and utility bills with a spotlight on pharmacists. *The Mathematics of Taxes* spotlights accountants. These books really bring the "real life" aspect of math to life.

 Whatever text is chosen, the risk of just using the workbook pages is a real one. Many a math program has met its demise when the teacher decides to skip "all that stuff" that is the lesson and just get the page done. For a child, this is analogous to teaching nature from a biology textbook and never going outside. The child may memorize and classify the knowledge but he has no intimate relationship with the science.

 I begin our day with math. Math cultivates several desirable habits in young students. It encourages orderliness, care, and logical thinking. It sets the tone for thoughtful reasoning. In our home, each day's math time includes a cumulative review, usually just a quick warm-up flash card session or computational game. Then we progress to the introduction of a new idea or further exploration of a recently introduced concept, using concrete materials. Usually, the children make some written record of new concepts on worksheets or in their notebooks. Occasionally, they will write or dictate narratives, something like a "lab report" following a "math experiment." Every day includes problem solving, both in the book and in real life. Every day also includes a page of computing for drill. We also do mental math and brainteasers. At least twice a week, we play math games as a family after dinner.

 Building a math program has been a stretch for me. I have been challenged by my children and by the world outside our home. I am increasingly convinced that ours is a mathematical world. We cannot be math-phobic or mathematically illiterate. Neither can our children.

❧ Words from the Wise ❧

If there is no perfect math textbook, what constitutes a good math program?

Leonie Westenberg, Australia

I think an eclectic approach is Charlotte Mason's approach to math in a nutshell. She did not just prescribe certain texts but talked about an approach. But neither did she take just an activity approach to Maths. When you read School Education, you see that math or arithmetic texts were suggested and used. They were not considered the only way to approach the subject. I love Charlotte Mason's description of using dominoes and then making paper problems in "Inconstant Kitty" (Volume 1 of the Charlotte Mason series). A combination approach, of book-work and manipulatives, adjusted for each child aligns beautifully with Charlotte Mason. My older boys loved **Carry On, Mr. Bowditch** when they were younger. It was a good Maths read aloud. I must read it with the younger ones. Another we liked, was **The Phantom Tollbooth** by Norton Juster. It is a fantasy about a mathematical land. Another to read to the young boys! My teenagers have liked Pappas' **The Joy of Mathematics**, which has been a good supplement to Saxon.

Linda McDonough, Virginia

There has been much research of late as to why Americans lag behind the rest of the world in math. What is especially disturbing is that our best math students do not fare well against the best math students in countries such as Germany and Japan. One study focused on the best math teachers in each country and how they taught. In America, dozens of problems are assigned daily. The teacher demonstrates how to do the problem and then the students practice. If a student gets stuck, the teacher goes to the place he got off track and demonstrates where he went wrong. Contrast this to Japan where the teacher starts the day by placing one unfamiliar math problem on the board and asks the students to figure it out. The students work individually or in groups until they either figure it out or are completely stumped — at which point the teacher gives them a hint. It is in this way that the students *truly learn to think, analyze, and reason as opposed to parrot back calculations. I was always good at math. I attribute much of this to having poor math teachers and bright peers. We were essentially forced to teach ourselves if we wanted to get good grades. We did and I still remember eighty percent of eighth-grade algebra.*

I remember grumbling to my dad back in junior high, "What is the point of algebra?" and he answered, "It teaches you to think logically." This is the point of true mathematics. Arithmetic is about memorizing facts, figures, and formulas, but true mathematics is about seeing the relationships between patterns and numbers in the universe. While arithmetic is important and time must be spent drilling essential facts, this is not math.

To best learn math, children must explore how numbers relate to each other and to the world around them. For example, manipulating fractions shouldn't be taught in isolation by giving rules as to how and when they can be added or multiplied. Rather they should be taught in relation to division, decimals, money, and a timeline. They should also be taught in the context of when they are used like in cooking or dividing a pie. It wasn't until I had been married for ten years that I learned the point of calculus (my husband uses it to graph the curves of stocks and other financial instruments). When we see the reason for learning something, we are more motivated and this allows us to make broader connections.

Children learn more from games and explorations than from a workbook. They also learn to love math as they build concepts in an enjoyable and meaningful way. Regardless of what curriculum one uses, games can be substituted or added to enrich your child's understanding and love of math.

Cindy Kelly, Texas

What has made all the difference here is that we only do very short math sessions (ten to fifteen minutes.) two to three times a week when we are doing math. I think what really was hard with Saxon was just how long he had to sit. I feel that any of them can be adapted to the Charlotte Mason approach if you use the curriculum as a tool; keep it short, and help with the new concepts; make them fun (manipulatives and games) and let them drill until they feel comfortable, while giving up the endless drill on concepts they already know; that is effective.

Blowing the Dust off History and Science

When children learn using living books, the content areas of the curriculum *become* the curriculum. In a traditional elementary school, "reading" is taught all morning; math right after lunch; science and social studies periodically at the end of the day. In a typical textbook-oriented home school, more history and science are studied but they are approached with an eye toward filling the child with facts.

A living-books curriculum uses the content areas — science and history — as the framework upon which learning is built. Language Arts are taught in the context of content — history, science, religion, and literature. Needless to say, these courses of study move well beyond "neighborhood helpers" and "why we need the rain forest." They also move beyond the facts. Literature reaches the heart of the child. It inspires him. It engenders enthusiasm for learning and a desire for discovery.

Children learn that history is the story of mankind and science is the story of his environment (in the broadest sense). Well-written literature offers both content and context. Together, both the parent educator and the pupil ponder deeply truth and fallacy. They consider God's hand on the world as it was and as it is. A*nd they are moved to consider His call regarding how it should be.*

Edith Stein reminds those who choose what to study that in a truly well-educated child the soul is of primary importance and the intellect is secondary. "I wish only to investigate education in respect to the soul. What materials does the soul need for development? It must receive something into itself in order to grow. And, as we have seen, only that which the soul receives internally can become an integral part of it so that we can speak of growth and formation; that which is received by senses and intellect remains an exterior possession." (*Woman*, 136)

There is a never-ending debate among home educators regarding whether history must be taught chronologically. I think this debate is silly. Unless the child is an only child, growing up isolated from the world, he will learn history out of order. Children learn history in the context of current events; they learn it when we celebrate national holidays; and they learn it from their siblings. They learn it when we celebrate the feast days of many, many saints, putting each life in its historical context. Typically, home educators are also concerned about "covering it all." You can't cover it all.

History is being made every day. Science expands and evolves with every breath. Instead of trying to cover it all, we can seek to enable the child to become intimate with what we do cover and to forge relationships with the characters and concepts that define our past and so determine our future. We can cover less but cover it far better.

I have spent hours agonizing over how to choose what we will study. I have worried about whether I can expose my children to everything necessary for cultural literacy. I have wondered how to avoid the inevitable holes in the education of seven children. Karen Andreola offers an analogy which put my mind at ease.

She suggests that parent educators ponder a hammock. There are holes, to be sure. But the rope is of the finest quality and it is tied tightly. The rope offers structure and function. The hammock is strong, despite the holes.

So, too, is a living education. A child forms relationships with the content because his education is integrated; he spends unhurried time interacting with the subject matter, reading it, writing about it, discussing it. This approach is a stark contrast to the conveyor belt education that is the norm in the United States today. The scope and sequence chart in a typical textbook looks impressive. There a lot of facts mentioned there and it looks like the child will learn a great deal. In reality, he will survey a great deal and look at nothing in detail.

Education is an art; it is not a science. There is no perfect method, perfectly applied, which will result in perfectly educated children. There is constant evaluation and adjustment. We cannot begin to outline at the beginning of kindergarten what we are determined to teach for the next twelve years. To do so would be to deny the possibilities of new ideas, new interests, new adventures. Instead, we accept that we cannot cover everything. We know that the holes are a part of the design, and that the design is an art.

We live in an age when information is readily available. Children need to learn how to retrieve information and what to do with it when they find it. They need to learn how to act creatively and ethically upon information. Schools concentrate on giving a child what he needs to pass the test; we can concentrate on training a child to think for a lifetime of learning, while also imparting vital information. We can train their minds, to be sure. More importantly, we can touch their hearts and souls.

Stone Wall at Gettysburg.

History

Any historical period is best studied using well-written whole books. Whether historical fiction or biography, the book should capture the imagination of the child and hold it, transporting the child back in time and to another place where he can truly learn about life as it was. The mark of a truly excellent book is the engagement of the full attention of the whole family. Even young children will listen attentively to material far above their reading level if the prose is engaging.

Focus on the people who shape history. Children care about people. They want to know who they were, how they lived, what they ate, how they felt, and what happened to them. Children need heroes, and history is full of stories of men and women used by God to do good in the world. The heroes of our history will inspire the hearts of our children and their stories will influence the future of our world. History will provide villains too, and there will be ample opportunity for you to use the examples of both to shape your child's understanding of good and evil.

Concentrate on the quality of the literature when making plans. Spend time with catalogs like Bethlehem Books (www.bethlehembooks.com), Sonlight (www.sonlight.com), and Greenleaf Press (www.greenleafpress.com) to familiarize yourself with what is available to reflect a particular time period. Read reviews of books online and in catalogs and forge a friendship with the children's librarian at your library. Be forewarned that there is excellent literature that is not written from a Catholic or even a Christian perspective. Young children, who cannot make judgments, should have books that are clearly noble. Older children can handle books that might contain profanities or less than noble ideas when those books are thoroughly discussed with the parent. There is value in the work, just as there is value in art at the hands of a gifted but not holy artist. Part of a child's education is learning to separate the wheat from the chaff, under the guidance of the parent educator.

Follow the sequence of events within a time period but do not be terribly concerned with telling the entire history story chronologically. The use of a timeline mounted on the wall is invaluable. As a child studies a person, he places a small drawing of that person on the timeline. Here, he can begin to conceptualize where a person figures in history. Don't limit timeline figures to history studies — artists, musicians, scientists, and saints should all be placed in context.

In our home, we concentrate on American history about once every three or four years, really delving deeply and studying it with an intensity fueled by interest and enthusiasm. There is an abundance of quality historical fiction pertaining to this time and place in history. Fluent readers have a book going all the time. Younger children listen to read-alouds read by Mom or Dad. Everyone narrates orally and draws pictures and cartoons. Older students produce written narrations. Dinner conversations frequently reflect ideas encountered in reading.

We take advantage of our proximity to historic Virginia and Washington, D.C., to go on frequent day trips and grand excursions. We don't leave the study there, languishing for years until time to study it formally comes around again. We revisit American history on holidays, shaping the minds of children through stories, songs, and celebrations. And we have frequent, unplanned daily reviews as we discuss current events in the context of history.

World history can be studied much the same way. Field trips are limited to museums and art galleries (though I certainly wouldn't rule out a trip abroad). Again, biographies and historical fiction are the cornerstones of our studies. Typically, ancient and European history is the focus of world history studies. In our home, care is taken to also explore the history of other world cultures such as those of China, Japan, India, the Middle East, Australia, Africa, and South America.

Americans have a very Western worldview. This is unfortunate since it is our calling to go out and make believers of all nations. This is not just an evangelical Protestant call. It is God calling us — faithful Catholics — to bring the Word and the Real Presence of Christ to all people of the world. We cannot begin to reach the large percentage of unevangelized peoples until we endeavor to understand their history. It is egocentric at best to believe that we can.

Certainly our children need to understand Western civilization, but they also need to understand non-Western cultures. The world has become increasingly smaller, and cultures clash every day, sometimes violently. Our schools don't truly teach our own history, and they certainly don't teach the history of other cultures. Multiculturalism, as it is trumpeted in schools, is largely superficial, just as American history is. In a living education, we seek understanding by studying history in context. In the case of studying non-Western cultures, we move beyond what is comfortable and familiar, to what is authentic, interesting, and enlightening. The Sonlight Curriculum catalog has countless suggestions of living books to use to teach multicultural history and language arts. They are captivating, winsome stories, written in excellent literary style. Pick and choose a few and study them Charlotte Mason–style.

I have found that even picture books can reflect authentic multiculturalism. For the discerning parent, there is a wealth of quality literature depicting all four corners of the world. These books are genuine living books and can be enjoyed by very young children and their older siblings. I've chosen some of the best of multi-cultural picture books for inclusion in the booklist at the back of this book. I use them with older children to teach a wide range of literary techniques. They are also natural jumping-off places for further research on geography and cultures of the world.

The booklist included at the end of this book suggests books upon which one can build a curriculum. While it is by no means inclusive, it is deep and varied enough to offer a rich spectrum of living ideas. Those books can be used to employ all the methods outlined in this book.

From the time they are very little, I teach my children to keep notebooks, journaling what they have learned in history. These notebooks become the Book of Centuries. At least once a week, I type their oral narrations for them to illustrate and to place in the notebook. The notebook is organized chronologically, in order to facilitate the child physically placing an event into the proper time period. Simply insert a tabbed divider for each century into the notebook. The child files narrations, maps, and other drawings behind the tabs. The organization will help them to develop a concept of time.

Children also illustrate during read-aloud time. The study of history frequently presents opportunities for drawing and studying maps. Geography is studied in context and retained by children of all ages because it has meaning. It is the study of the land and of the people who inhabit the land. The geography of a country is relevant because we make connections about the role it played in the history of the people who live there and the role it continues to play today. Of course, the maps are treasured and preserved in the notebooks.

I cannot begin to characterize adequately what this approach to teaching "social studies" has done in our family. I think of the watered-down textbooks in a typical school and I am genuinely sorry for the children who grow up believing that they represent the social studies. Last fall, while driving four hours to a soccer tournament, my children and I listened to a recording of *On To Oregon* by Honore Morrow. The story is one of the Sager family, seven children orphaned on the Oregon Trail. Henry Sager, the eldest, is a fourteen-year-old boy who promises his dying mother that he will care for the six-week-old baby as if it were his own child and that he will keep his family together. It is a true story of their difficult journey and their ultimate triumph. The story is so gripping that when we arrived at our destination, my children didn't want to get out of the car; they wanted to keep listening.

When we arrived home, my eldest, an eleven-year-old boy, wrote a lengthy narration. He also exhibited a curious attitude of cheerful, responsible tenderness toward his younger siblings that I can only attribute to the example of Henry Sager. The younger children took our wagon from the garage and played Oregon Trail for days on end. Granola bars became pemmican; the dog was recruited to be a horse; and baby dolls were pressed into service by a seven-year-old boy who heretofore wouldn't be caught dead with a doll. This was narration done very well. The story had touched the hearts of all the children who heard. It touched their mother as well, haunting me for weeks and inspiring gratitude for the luxuries of modern life we so often take for granted.

That is but one example of a living-books education. We learned a great number of facts about the pioneers. They are imprinted in our minds in rich, descriptive language. But we learned even more about the human spirit, and that lesson is imprinted on our hearts and tucked into our souls.

Science

In many ways, it is impossible to separate history from science. The scientists who have contributed to our understanding of the world are historical figures. And their discoveries have shaped our history. In a relevant science education, relationships are constantly being recognized and intimacies with the natural world are formed.

I consider two components to my children's science education. They are inextricably intertwined. The first is the knowledge and understanding they gain through living books. The second is the knowledge and understanding they gain through personal contact with the natural world.

In our home, we are always engrossed in at least one science book. That book may be a well-written nonfiction book on a particular content area, a biography of a scientist, a natural-history book, or a fictional book with a focus on things scientific. Some books, like those written by Holling C. Holling or Gene Stratton Porter, I read aloud to all the children. Some are read by a child individually, as dictated by his interests.

The books are not textbooks. Charlotte Mason writes, "Books dealing with science…should be of literary character, and we should probably be more scientific as a people if we scrapped all the text books which swell publishers' lists and nearly all the chalk expended so freely on our chalkboards." (*Philosophy of Education*, 218)

I require careful narrations of these books and spend much time discussing their content. The narrations, if they are oral, are recorded by me and kept in the child's science notebook. Written narrations are also kept. Occasionally, one of these books will lend itself to some experimentation. We write up lab reports and keep them in notebooks too. Almost always, the books beg to be illustrated. Even if they are published with illustrations, my children long to put on paper the pictures in their minds. These pictures are priceless additions to the science notebooks.

I try to have a general plan for science study for the year. I look at each year in six-week increments, considering seven such blocks of time per year. During each six-week period, I try to focus on one particular aspect of science education. Typical "units" include botany, animal science, astronomy, chemistry, physics, geology, human anatomy and physiology, and marine biology. I rotate through the disciplines, adding others as the need arises. I force myself to be relaxed about this study — I don't want to kill science by being a slave to a schedule of readings. I gear the study to the time of year:

we consider marine biology in the summer, and we might study botany both in the spring and the fall of the same year, since the plant world is very different in different seasons.

It is crucial that the reader understand the purpose behind the planned bookwork: I seek to provide a foundation upon which the child will build his understanding of the natural world. Nature study in the field is essential and integral to this method of teaching science. The child will learn much about the world in the context of excellent, living science books. Little of it will be "real" for him until he goes out and forms relationships in the world the good Lord created for him to enjoy. It is the processing time, in the field, interacting with science on a very personal level, that teaches the child the most. Galileo wrote, "You cannot teach anyone anything. You can only help them to discover it within themselves." To facilitate such self-education, a cycle of book study using living texts, fieldwork, and more book study (focused this time to bring the fieldwork into clearer view) is encouraged over and over again throughout childhood.

Nature study does not seem to come naturally to most mothers. They are uncertain about what to do and how to do it. I have found the "One Small Square" series of books by Donald Silver to be an invaluable resource for showing parents and children alike how to explore the natural world. All the books in the world, however, are of little use unless one is willing to pack up and get outside. Once the effort is made, the rewards are remarkable.

MacBeth Derham, who has the distinction of being a professional naturalist as well as a home educating mother, describes such an excursion:

1. *I like to have a place we go often. Find a place near you that is free and close. This makes it easy to frequent the place, and you will get a good feel for seasonal changes and differences. The park we have chosen is a huge old estate with several environments, including forest, field, seashore, and pond. There are maps and well-marked trails.*
2. *Bring the things you need. Have a checklist if you need to, since nothing spoils a field study quicker than missing equipment. And don't forget water and snacks, especially in the hotter months.*
3. *Have the children carry their own stuff. We have separate nature backpacks for each child. They keep pencils, notebooks, magnifying lenses, bug boxes, small dip nets, zippered freezer bags, magnets, small field guides, self-adhesive labels, and a compass...lots of good stuff! We also bring larger dip nets and insect nets, binoculars...*
4. *I usually have a Peterson's guide for species identification. These are heavy for the children, so I bring them.*
5. *Karen Andreola talks about "Mom" sitting on a blanket and waiting for the children to find nature goodies and bring them to her. Sometimes I do this, but more often I am as interested in the "finding" as they are. Keeping a blanket area as a "base camp" (unless you're hiking) will give the children a place to sit while drawing.*
6. *Bring your enthusiasm. It may be hard to get excited about seaweed or deer droppings, but even a little parental excitement goes a long way.*
7. *Be on the lookout for the "teachable moment." If you have planned a tree study, and a herd of deer is browsing in the woods, forget the trees for a few moments!! I was teaching survival skills to a group once when a golden eagle (very rare here) perched on a dead tree just above us, for about twenty minutes, preening. Survival switched to ornithology.*
8. *Plan a few activities. Younger children like scavenger hunts and bingo (each child has a card with several different animals...find five across first to win). Older children could do classifications hunts...how many phyla*

are represented? How many different species of crab live here? Videotape mud snails looking for food, or the undulating motion of night crawlers. Press flowers.

9. Follow up with sketching in nature notebooks, taking photos, reading about the flora and fauna in greater depth, or organizing a collection...

A nature notebook, filled with drawings and descriptions of discoveries becomes a personal diary of growth for a child. Looking back upon what he has encountered, what he has learned, and what touched him, he begins to understand himself a little better and he is drawn ever closer to his Creator. We have loosely organized these notebooks by discipline and then by taxonomy within the life sciences.

It is helpful to plan a nature walk once a week. At first, that sounds daunting. Home educators have so much to do. "There is so much scope and sequence to cover." Remember, we are not to be slaves to scope and sequence. Try to get out at the same time almost every week, regardless of the weather. As a matter of fact, the weather and the seasons are part of the study. The pond looks very different on a snowy winter afternoon than it does on a sweltering summer day. This outing might be the most important half-day of the entire week. From this outing, you will find countless rabbit trails (both literally and figuratively). With the exception of Mass, nothing is more important to a child's education.

Don't look on nature study as something to cross off your "to do" list, look at it as food for your soul — and your child's. This is your chance to kick a stone along a wooded path or to skip it across a creek. It is an opportunity to bundle up children in pajamas on a clear winter night to gaze at the stars. A nature walk will offer you endless opportunities for lively discussion and equal opportunities for reverent silence.

The Clarksons write, "Your goal in nature study, though, is much more than just to 'inform' your children about the details of creation. Your greater task is to 'form in' them eyes that can see the Creator in his creation (Romans 1:20), an abiding sense of wonder and appreciation of what God has made (Psalms 8 and 19) and a passion to care for, subdue and rule over this earth as God's highest expression of created being (Genesis 1: 28)." (*Educating The WholeHearted Child*, 124) You won't find this goal on any scope and sequence chart. Yet, it is a goal that no child should fail to attain. It is true education.

Nowhere do history and nature come together so beautifully as in our country's national parks. There, a family adventure waits to unfold, and a whole world of diverse history and science begs to be explored. From the seashore of Cape Cod to the swamps of the Florida Everglades to the lush forests of Shenandoah to the vast landscape of the Grand Canyon, our country's history comes alive in her national parks. My children have made it their goal to visit all of them. My husband and I have made it our goal to help them reach their goal! I can't emphasize enough the importance of outdoor education as a family. For further reading on the topic, I heartily recommend *Adventuring with Children* by Nan Jeffrey.

I leave you with two more narrations. One is the very first written narration attempted by Elizabeth Derham, MacBeth's nine-year-old daughter. It is entirely unedited. Even the poetry at the beginning was the child's idea. The second is my son Michael's narration of a recent camping trip to Shenandoah National Park. In both narrations, the integrity of the child's education is clear. They are articulate; their writing is clear and unaffected, but rich in imagery. More than that, they are inspired. Libby and Michael are writing about something about which they care and something with which they are intimate.

**Lost in the Woods
A True Story
By Elizabeth Derham**

*"In Autumn down the beechwood Path
The leaves lie thick upon the ground.
It's there I love to kick my way
And hear their crisp and crashing sound…"*

James Reeves

My name is Elizabeth Derham. My companions were Mary, Lydia, Annika, Donald, and Paul. My mom and her friend Karen were with me, too. On November 1st, 1999, we entered the Red Triangle trail at the north end of the parking lot at Harriman State Park. As we came in, I spotted a medium sized rock. We climbed it. I almost slipped off its scratchy surface. We moved on to different rocks. We climbed rocks nearly perpendicular to the ground. We found two ways to get up to the top (it turned out that there was a champagne bottle on top). We found plenty of caves on our way up, and everyone (except me) climbed through one.

Climbing more rocks, with blueberry bushes on either side, we came to a bluff. Mary, Lydia, and I climbed on it. Nearby, Donald found another bluff. We climbed that one, too, and Annika followed. "Ooh!" said Mary. "Ahh!" said Annika. There was an exquisite view from there. There were beautiful trees of fall colors and the sky was so blue! We saw three of the seven lakes. My mother said they looked like two eyes with curly-q hair. Then, we stored the view in our memory boxes so we could keep them forever. We marched on. The forest was getting thicker now and the hike was getting harder. There were fewer and fewer rocks. We found a tree trunk fallen across a pile of rocks and decided to use it as a seesaw. It worked well!

Donald ran off because he wanted to try out our new walkie-talkies. My mom called him back. We lost one of our walkie-talkies, as we hiked on.

After a while, we came to a creek running through the forest. Jumping over it was not a problem, for most of us, but Paul was too scared. Mom had to carry him. We crossed over two more creeks on the way and one of them had a big root "sculpture" crossing over and under itself. Nearby, we saw a bird's nest. Now we were on the Yellow Square trail, and there were mine trails, and old cellars filled with water.

Mary put her stick inside a cellar pit filled with water (it was deep). We went on and on, going up and going down, but the road was mostly clear and flat because we were on an actual trail called the Dunning Road. Now we were on a flat road running on the edge of the mountain, and Mary and I started to get ahead.

By now, Mary and I were quite ahead, and we came to a fork in the road. We remembered the yellow trail markers, and followed them to the left. When, we came to a valley with a little stream in the middle, Mary said, "Aren't we getting ahead?" "No," I said. "Well, I'm going back!" said Mary, and Mary went back. I heard noises in the distance, and I began to get worried.

I looked back and discovered that no one was there, and I started to run back like lightening. It turned out that the others were a quarter of a mile behind me. At first, my mom was mad at me for having gone ahead. After what I had to say about feeling lost, no one was really angry.

Now the rocks were much smaller. Lydia stumbled over the biggest one. We were deep — very, very, deep — in the forest. My mom looked in her map book as we stuffed our pockets full of moss for our snails back home. Mom said we had to retreat since we had missed a turn. It was quite dull to go over hills that we had already gone over, but Karen started to sing to lift up our spirits. Songs made me feel better!

We finally got to a trail called the Turquoise trail. We came to a very damp area and I missed a rock as we were crossing it. It was getting dark, and harder to see the trail. Since Karen is legally blind, she tripped a lot. By now, though, none of us could see a thing. My mom tried to look in her book, but she couldn't see the words. She looked carefully on the trees for markers, and found two. We kids were trying to figure out a way to sleep if we had to stay the night.

After a while, Mom said to go up a hill that looked like it had a path leading up it. The hill was covered with mountain laurel bushes. They were scratching everybody in the legs and arms, and one was so tall it scratched my face. Then, Mom announced that we were lost! We hadn't seen another person in over 2 hours. Everything was totally quiet except the crunch of leaves...

"Look!" someone shouted, and I don't know who said it, but there in the dark was a faint light. "Maybe it's a shiny tiger," said Donald with alertness. No way," I said, "That must be somebody." As we looked, the light got brighter and eventually it actually passed us. That is when he heard us cry, "We are looking for the turquoise trail!" "You're not on it!" a taunting voice answered. "Follow the light," he continued. We followed it through the mountain laurel, which scratched our arms and knees more, until we got to a guy with the light. He had a headlamp on, so we couldn't see his face. His name was Kevin.

The hike to the parking lot took a grueling hour. We had already been hiking for four hours before Kevin found us. One of the facts I gathered there was that there are always rocks before a stream around here. We went on and on, and our legs were very tired. We lost the trail twice. Kevin says I have good eyes, and he wants to come on our next hike!

I could see the Seven Lakes Drive, now. Annika saw a swampy place, and we got our sneakers wet. We found a river, and Kevin had to carry Paul and Annika across it.

On our way out, we saw some deer. Kevin saw them first. I've never seen so many stars and constellations. We looked at them for a while, until it was time to go. We stopped at Dunkin' Donuts where I got a donut with chocolate sprinkles. Then we all went home. I'll never forget that hike!

Camping in Shenandoah National Park
by Michael Foss

We got a late start on Wednesday because MacBeth got stuck in traffic. As soon as the Derhams got to our house, we left, heading west for a great adventure at Shenandoah National Park. We got on Skyline Drive at Front Royal and started our audio tour. The day was cool and cloudy and sometimes we couldn't see at all because we were driving in a cloud.

We traveled all the way to milepost 41 to the Limberlost Trail. This trail was named for the Gene Stratton Porter novel, The Girl of the Limberlost. It is an easy trail because it has crushed green gravel for wheelchair accessibility. The trees were mixed; some were still green and some had already changed to fall colors. We had a picnic lunch as soon as we got there and Christian got stung by a wasp. He didn't even cry but his neck did swell up and it sure did hurt.

On the trail, Christian and Trip saw a chipmunk. We saw a salamander in the creek and we caught it to look at it for a few minutes. Then we let it go because you are only allowed to keep what you are going to eat. Nobody wanted to eat salamander. There was lichen on the trees. One log had lots of lichen and right next to it were a bunch of trees in full fall color. Michael sketched that. All the trees were huge, old hemlocks.

After we left Limberlost, we went to Big Meadows. At Big Meadows, there is a campground, a lodge, a store and cabins. We checked into our cabin and got all our stuff out of the car. Then we went to find the Derhams campsite. When we got there, they were already all set up. We helped start a fire to make dinner. We gathered wood and milkweed. Milkweed is a great fire starter. We also burned all the remnants of the Derhams Happy Meal dinner from the day before. We gathered all the coals and put them on one side of the fire pit. MacBeth stoked the fire.

We boiled broth for chicken soup. MacBeth had already cooked the chicken and the broth came in a box. She added some vegetables, including Trip's garden turnips. We put potatoes in foil right on the coals. Mom forgot the butter so when the potatoes were done, we added them to the soup.

While we were cooking the soup, five deer were just off our campsite. When we went towards them, they didn't run away. Instead, they came to visit. We think they thought we would feed them. We didn't because the deer can die much sooner if they eat people food. Annika began to keep track of how many deer we saw on the trip. We got up to twenty-eight before the trip's end. Libby found a humongous fungus! It was elephant ear fungus.

We were starving and the soup was delicious. Annika added half a bottle of salt to hers. It was not delicious. While we ate soup, the steak was cooking. MacBeth put a batch of cookie dough in a tin pan and put it in a tin lobster pot with a lid on the fire and the cookies baked. All this time, Michael kept the fire going. We roasted marshmallows and ate steak at the same time. And we had warm fire-roasted cookies. Everything was delicious! It was pretty cold by then, but Libby warmed her hands enough to play some violin. She was awesome.

Before dark, we had to be really careful to clean up all our food and utensils so the bears wouldn't come into our campsite. The bears at Shenandoah are black bears. Usually, the teenage bears go after the food because they don't know any better. If you see a bear, you should not make eye contact. Wave your arms over your head and yell at the bear (or pray real loudly). Black bears are not nearly as ferocious as grizzlies. There are no grizzlies in Shenandoah and we wanted to see a black bear but not up too close.

When it was dark, after Stephen had eaten for about two hours, he got cranky. Mom said it was time to go to our cabin. The boys begged to stay in the tent and MacBeth said that was just fine. Michael and Christian had warm L.L. Bean sleeping bags. Patrick says he was very cold in a go-to-grandma's sleeping bag. Everybody slept in his clothes (which smelled like smoke). Just as we were going to sleep, we heard and saw an animal rubbing against the side of the tent. MacBeth went to investigate and the mysterious visitor turned out to be a dog named "Buddy." Whew! We had thought maybe it was a bear!

We went to sleep all huddled together and we thought those hot water bottles were a very good idea. It was very dark out there. Mom and Mary Beth and Stephen slept all warm and snug in the cabin. Mom said something about not wanting to leave us alone in a tent while she hiked to the bathroom three times a night. Wimps!

When we woke up, we all trundled into the Volvo and went to the cabin. We all took warm showers. Mom checked out of the cabin and we returned to the campsite to start breakfast. We tried to start the fire without a match but we gave up when we decided we were too hungry for that nonsense. The menu called for bacon and eggs cooked in a brown lunch bag. First you take two strips of bacon and line the bottom of the bag. Then you poke a stick through the bag at the top and hold it over the fire until the bacon fat coats the bag bottom. The trick is to hold it close enough to melt the bacon but not so close that the bag catches fire. Trip's bag caught fire immediately. Michael was not far behind Trip. Patrick was extremely careful and patient and sat there for close to an hour, melting his bacon. Then he put an egg on top and cooked that. He says it was good but next time he'd just as soon use a frying pan.

Michael and Trip, when they discovered there were no more bags, got inventive. They cooked their bacon in the bottom of tin cans. Then they added eggs and cooked those on top. It was greasy but good.

In the meantime, Mom lined pans with more bacon and put sliced leftover potatoes on top. We cooked this in MacBeth's lobster pot oven. Right next to our campsite, we discovered an apple tree. Mom had just mixed pancake batter which quickly became cobbler topping. She sliced apples from the tree, put them in a pan, poured maple syrup and apple pie spice (MacBeth thought of everything — even pie spice) on top and then put the pancake batter on top. This baked in that lobster pot oven until it was just perfect apple cobbler. It tasted great with MacBeth's hot chocolate. Martha Stewart would be proud of those two moms. At last, we finished our two hour breakfast adventure.

It was time to go to Dark Hollow Falls for a hike. From the time we started, we could see a valley as we hiked along the trail. The valley was created by the small stream that would eventually become the eighty foot waterfall. The trees were already in their fall colors and were very pretty. Halfway through the hike, there was a small stream that pooled a little and we could see a bunch of small trout, about six inches long. We stayed there for a while and climbed on the rocks and Michael almost caught a trout. Instead of catching one, he got stuck between a rock and a log in the water. Libby and Christian had to help Michael turn himself right side around and get off the log. Paul was leading the pack the whole way down the trail. Near the falls, we saw a huge mountainside rock the size of the whole side of the house. All kinds of different algae and weird black fungus grew there.

When we got to the falls, it was really amazing. Trip climbed up the rocks. He would have climbed all the way up the waterfall if MacBeth hadn't stopped him. Michael decided to start swinging from tree limbs. Then we hiked a little farther down the waterfall. We saw another small waterfall. When we were exploring that, Patrick saw more trout and fish and told everyone about it. Then we decided to turn around and go back up the trail.

Going up was much harder and we had to practically drag Paul. On the way up, some people told us to look for deer on the cliffside. We didn't find any. Some other people wanted to know if we were the group with two ladies camping alone with all those kids. Actually, it was only nine kids, ten including Nicholas, "camping" in Mom's belly.

Trip and Christian found two caterpillars. One was a wooly bear caterpillar. The other was a black and white wooly caterpillar with black spikes.

They caught the caterpillars for Mary Beth, who loves caterpillars. In the car, Mary Beth took the caterpillar out of the jar and let it crawl all over her hands. It was really beautiful. She put it back into the jar. About three minutes later, she started screaming. Her hands were red and puffy and they hurt her.

Michael took her to the bathroom to wash her hands and Mom and MacBeth went in search of Benadryl. Libby and Michael took the caterpillar, in the jar, to the park rangers. The ranger said it was a Hickory Tussock Moth caterpillar and that some people are allergic to its hairs. Mary Beth was clearly one of those people. We gave her some medicine and went back to camp. She was pretty pitiful for a little while. Mom and MacBeth both wondered aloud exactly how far we were from a hospital.

We started the fire again and roasted hotdogs on a stick and ate salsa and chips for lunch. The hotdogs were much easier to cook than the bacon and eggs. Washing dishes was tricky because there was only cold water in the bathrooms and at the pumps. We had to heat the water on the fire. Still, it was better than doing dishes at home. Actually, everything was better than at home. I guess the trip counts as school, but it sure didn't feel that way. It felt better than a day at the best amusement park.

We reluctantly left the Derhams to begin our journey home. Michael and Christian and Patrick begged to stay but MacBeth didn't have room in the car. Mom said next time, we'd bring our own big tent and camping gear and bring Dad. When we got home, Daddy was there. He said he had never seen Stephen look so dirty. He also said we all smelled like smoke. We went off to take warm baths and discovered we had no hot water. If there's no hot water at home, what's the point? We want to go back to Shenandoah next week!

Words from the Wise

A conversation with MacBeth Derham, outdoor educator from New York

I bought a textbook, and we go outside. How do I help my children to encounter things in an orderly manner?

One thing the children might enjoy, and help to put things in order in their minds, might be learning to make their own "keys." Take a series of objects and determine what makes each thing different from or similar to the other objects. There is a specific format for this. Here is part of a key that the children did for the fauna in our yard. Keying is also a form of logic study, and is the basis for computer language — lots of "if...then" statements.

#1. a. If it has feathers, go to #2.
     b. If it has no feathers, go to #3.

#2. a. If red, it is a cardinal
     b. If it is not red, go to #4.

#3. a. If it has a bushy tail, it is a squirrel.
     b. If it has no bushy tail, go to #5.

Etc.

One of the biggest detriments to some approaches is that the children appear to study huge amounts of content but they live very little of it. How can we help here? Is there a way to blend book-work and field study?

The balance here is crucial. Which is supplementing which? Does the book-work supplement the fieldwork, or vice versa? I realize that some things may never be discovered in a nature walk, but can we build a "home-study-program" where there is a perfect complement of field and book-work? Do your resources include a range of living book recommendations? My house is full of science texts, workbooks, etc. Most are awful. Many have major errors. Maybe one will be useful for high school chemistry.

One of the things I like about using National Geographic *on CD-Rom is the index. I might use a science text as a study guide, and then find the articles I need on the subject quickly with the handy index...it is much faster than thumbing through issue after issue. This way, though, they miss the "browse factor," that is, distraction by other articles, which always lead me to learning more about other subjects...if you follow my meaning here. I do keep several years' worth kicking about the house for just this reason. I guess it is sort of the "teachable moment" of the written word.*

Short of moving to New York City and going with you on every mountain day, how can I be certain that my children have an excellent nature education, so that it is the strong foundation of all else?

Is there a naturalist/mentor you know who could help? I have always been one to pick the brains of other hikers for information. Another thing I like to do is keep a notebook with a simple list of all the species I have identified. As the list grows, one becomes more intimate with nature. Weren't Adam and Eve given the task of naming all the animals? And names mean things, so in collecting names one is also collecting facts and ideas. This helps make connections.

Science needs to be "hands-on." Can it be hands-on and structured without burnout?

I find that my children find their fieldwork a pleasant relief from book-work, and thus might get more out of it...maybe.

One of the (many) things I remember with great pleasure from a recent visit to a homeschooling friend's house is her son's enthusiasm as he caught fish in a creek. I watched him and mentally noted all the things he was learning about science: fish behavior, color, habitat; patience; perseverance;

technique; observation skills, etc. He felt the cold water, slipped on the algae-covered rocks, and still figured out how to catch those wiggly little fish. Like most children, he is a born scientist. I would have a hard time imagining his enthusiasm with the Christian Liberty science workbook, or even a good Catholic science text. He is so blessed to have a mom who recognizes the value of field experience.

Here are a few of my thoughts on structure in science:

What if you had planned a day of birding on that walk, and he had seen the fish and wanted to catch them. Would you have seen this as disrupting your science lesson? Suppose he wanted to catch fish every time you visited that place, no matter what you had planned (scientists often must repeat the same experiments, and a good naturalist makes many observations). Would you recognize the value of each nature walk, even if your plans were changed? These are the concerns I have when it comes to organizing science.

Recall Charlotte Mason's words on the object lesson: "Object-lessons should be incidental; and this is where the family enjoys a great advantage over the school. The child who finds that wonderful and beautiful object, a 'paper' wasp's nest…has his lesson on the spot from father or mother…It is unnecessary in the family to give an exhaustive examination to every object…"(Parents and Children, 182–183). I am so inclined to agree with her, on this matter, more than anything else in her books. When we ignore the teachable moment for our own plans we send two messages. One is that the child's interests are unimportant. The other is that plans can't be changed. I despise both of these messages; the first is simply the sinful disregard for others, while the second promotes inflexibility in thinking that destroys scientific thought! Remember the story of Alexander Fleming and the hunt for antibiotics? He had a plan, but something (bread mold) kept killing his bacterial specimens! How could he find something that would kill his bacteria if they kept dying on him? Thinking beyond his plan brought on a revolution in medicine. The great "Aha!" of science must be found, and is rarely taught.

But what if my child always wants to catch fish, and never observes anything else?

In the simple process of catching fish, there is so much value in what he is doing. You see, in his mind I believe he is quietly noting the different days, how difficult the fish are to find, how many there are, if the weather makes a difference, what tools work best, etc. He is slowly building his own scientific database on these fish. When he has all he feels he needs, he will move on. This may take some time. Scientists are patient. Their mothers must be, too. (Jane Goodall was in Gombe for thirty years — and by the way, she had no scientific background except keen observations skills learned in her childhood from making connections with nature). A child's passion for catching these fish is pure science. He is discovering everything about the fish as if he were the first person ever to observe them! Think about that! Can any text or guide come close to providing him with that kind of experience?

When given the time and opportunity to explore the natural world as if he were the first person to ever see it, he is learning to become a naturalist. Even when I was working full-time as a naturalist, I wished I had taken the college courses after my fieldwork because the classroom lectures were a jumble of terms and names and were meaningless to me. I learned more "on the job" in a month than I learned in four years of biology and chemistry. classes.

My son just finished studying plant reproduction. While gardening, I asked him some questions about how plants reproduce. When he gave the wrong answers, he saw my face fall. Now he says he hates science. I do need better books — "living" fact books. How do I rekindle a love for science in him?

Oh, dear! Death of a naturalist! Let's try and revive him.

Textbooks are full of facts. The realization that children soak up ideas and concepts, as well as facts, should be a guide to lesson planning. A living book provides the substance, ideas, and concepts that make the facts stick with the children. Experience is also key, and though many curricula suggest a slew of boxed experiments and books on experiments, I just don't think all that is necessary. Now, how do we inspire a discouraged child? I think there are several things you can do. Introduce some living history books which include science...sort of a sneaky back way to helping him connect with his inner naturalist. You probably have books like **Archimedes and the Door of Science**, but how about **Diary of an Early American Boy**? This book is full of illustrations of life on a farm in 1805, and includes agriculture, machines and weather. **Farmer Boy** also has some great weather and agriculture. Remember the section on frost, where the whole family had to get up in the middle of the night and try and save the potato crop before sunrise? Or how about **Sugartime: The Hidden Pleasures of Making Maple Syrup With a Primer for the Novice Sugarer** (whew!) by Susan Carol Hauser. It has a lot of Native American lore, and plenty of info on trees and sugaring. **My Side of the Mountain** is another great read, with plenty of nature study. After you read this, you can make acorn pancakes! Yum! My son really enjoys the DK pocket series...in fact, he has asked for fifteen titles for Christmas, and was kind enough to figure out the cost for me. DK books of any size are full of information that is easy to digest. Are they living? I'm not sure, but they are engaging, and don't take up too much space. Sure, they offer bare facts, but the terrific photos help to connect the facts to the natural world.

Avoid quizzing. Rather than asking, "How do you think this plant reproduces?" comment on the size and quantity of the bulbs, and speculate on next year's flowers. Talk about the way the plant captured the sun's energy, and stored it up into the bulbs. This will help to reinforce a concept he has learned, rather than put him on the spot. I think that learning as a conversation between people (narration) should take the place of read-and-quiz. By engaging him with your thoughts on the matter, you help to build the crucial relations between his reading and reality. Quizzing changes the nature lesson. It is now no longer a chance to learn. This is probably more John Holt than Charlotte Mason, but I have no doubt that what he wrote in **How Children Fail** is right on the money.

What about experiments?

For experiments, we do have some kits-in-a-box from time to time, but the children often miss the point when everything is provided for them. My son wanted a kit called "Surf Frogs" for Christmas...a well-packaged frog habitat made of plastic, which comes with a mail-order frog voucher. It is rather expensive, so I suggested that in the spring, we go to a pond and catch some tadpoles. He then suggested that he could build his own frog habitat. He thought it would be fun to watch the "surprise," since we would not know what species our frog would be until it matured. And we could release it into its childhood home. The more natural method seemed more appealing.

Experiment books that I like include: **What?, Science for Kids: 39 Easy Astronomy Experiments** *and* **Science for Kids: 39 Easy Chemistry Experiments**, *all by Robert Wood. His books are a bit "cookbook-like," but he includes wonderful suggestions for independent study. Janice van Cleave's books are also popular with many homeschooling families.*

It has been my experience that there is little difference between one experiment book and another, especially for younger children. They all seem to have the "make a cloud in a bottle," "watch ice freeze" and "measuring rainfall" kind of basic experiments. All of these activities can be done easily without any science experiment book — and can often be done better through observing nature. One book I like that is not really a science experiment book is **Glues, Brews and Goos** *by Diana Marks. This is full of recipes for fun, art, science, geography, and more. There are no explanations; you and your children are left to ponder the results. This is a book that will encourage thinking. And isn't that the whole point of science education?*

Why should I bother to immerse myself and my family in a "living" historical fiction book like *Little House on the Prairie*? I don't want to go back to living the way they did in the olden days. Is this method of education relevant?

Lissa Peterson, Virginia

The Little House books give us a close, loving look at a close, loving family. It's that warm, cooperative, strong family life, with the merry moments around Pa's fiddle, the thrills of his stories, Ma's calm confidence through all kinds of trials, the overcoming of hardship together — it's all this that makes us fall in love with the Ingalls family. That exploration of a solid, loving, principled family is most certainly relevant to "real life." Love of family is, I think, at the heart of the desire to homeschool. Because you love your children so much, you want to give them the best education, the happiest childhood, the strongest moral and spiritual foundation, and you perceive that homeschooling — keeping the family together — is the best way to achieve those goals. The Ingallses serve as a model for us — not because they are homesteaders, but because they are a strong family. Even those devoted to the public school system cannot dispute the importance of a happy home life for their pupils. So yes, the Ingalls family as a role model has great relevance to real life.

Doing an author study — or following rabbit trails of interest — on the Little House books does not in any way mean that we homeschoolers are all longing for a return of ninteenth century technology. I thank God for my washing machine. I like reading about how Ma makes cheese, but it doesn't make me yearn to go through that process on a regular basis myself. I certainly don't want to slaughter my own pig to get my bacon. I have churned butter, and it was delicious on the johnny cake I baked in an iron stove — but I wouldn't want to get my butter that way all the time. It's time-consuming and hard on the arms. And that iron stove was a serious pain to use — not to mention all the cow chips I had to gather for the fire. I learned a lot from these experiences, and one of the largest lessons was gratitude for the many conveniences I take for granted. I also learned some science, some nutrition, some history. Again, subjects which all have great relevance in the "real world."

Yes, I do have spells of wishing I could have my own little frame house out in the country, with miles of beautiful land around me. But I wished the same thing when I was a student in public school — it's not strictly a homeschooler's longing. Often one of the first things a person will do when he strikes it rich is go out and buy a lot of land. I'm betting Bill Gates has some beautiful acres around his house, and he's about as high-tech as it gets. The longing for natural beauty, for unspoiled nature, for "country living," seems to be a perpetual one in mankind, no matter how technologically advanced we become. Isn't that one of the great benefits trumpeted by the Internet businesses — the luxury of working from home, from remote locations? Picture all those cell phone commercials that show people dialing into the office from the middle of the ocean or the wilds of Alaska.

If I ever do get that little house in the country, it will have a washing machine and electric lights and a cable modem. And yes, sometimes we'll turn out the lights and have a fire and candles. We won't watch much television — nor do we now — but that has more to do with our moral beliefs than a rejection of modern technology. It's modern morals I object to, not modern conveniences.

*And how about those rabbit trails? What do we actually LEARN from the Little House books? A lot about American history — westward expansion, the building of the railroads, the growth of Midwestern towns. How things were made, how things were done, how people dressed. Science — agricultural practices (compare them to modern methods); weather; spread of disease (fever 'n' ague in **Little House on the Prairie**); kitchen science; effects of technological advances (in **Little House in the Big Woods**, Laura is proud of Pa for being a pioneer in the use of the harvesting machine — that was cutting-edge technology); and lots more. All of this is stuff you'd (in theory) learn in a public-school classroom. We, however, find the living-literature approach to be a more effective conduit for this knowledge.*

One reason Laura Ingalls wrote her books is because she lived in a time of tremendous technological advances. She saw the advent of the washing machine (which she thought a most wonderful invention), the airplane, the

[115]

automobile, the telephone, and a whole lot of other stuff. She embraced these modern developments; you can read about her excitement over certain inventions in some of her essays and letters. But she also saw that a way of life was disappearing — that before long the simple tasks of daily life which had so occupied her family's time and energy during her childhood would be made obsolete by modern technology. And she believed that it was important that those "old-time" struggles and challenges be remembered.

Laura Ingalls Wilder believed you couldn't properly appreciate the miracles of modern technology if you had nothing with which to compare them. She said she wrote the Little House books to preserve a record of a way of life that was fast disappearing. She didn't say she wished it would stay — she saw the good in many modern developments — but she did wish that the values that seemed to go hand in hand with that earlier way of life might be preserved, cherished, maintained. She recognized that modern conveniences allowed people much more leisure time, and also that when things come easily they are likely to be taken for granted. The increase in leisure time taught people to expect pleasure and recreation as a right and gradually we have become a nation of pleasure-seekers who complain about work. Also, our leisure time activities became rather age-segregated. What is appropriate for Mom and Dad to watch on television isn't appropriate for the children. Give the children their own television and everyone's happy. Laura believed, and I heartily concur, that something wholesome and rich and lovely was lost when family members began to scatter each to their own entertainments. What many of us homeschoolers are talking about when we describe "returning to a more simple life" is a return to a lifestyle that centers around the family as a together unit. We gather in the evenings to read aloud, play games, pray, perhaps watch a movie together. We opt out of the frantic rush from activity to activity. We use our computers as learning tools, not so much as entertainment. Ditto our televisions and VCRs. We find pleasure in making bread from scratch, because we have time to do this with our children. But we still shop at the grocery store for sliced bread.

Are we trying to live back in time instead of preparing our children for the age in which we live? I don't think we're trying to live back in time. We're studying the past that we may learn from it and preserve what seems to us good and useful, in order to raise children who are most excellently prepared to stand strong and brave in the modern world. We are trying to prepare our children for the age in which we live. We want them to cherish family the way Laura Ingalls did; we want them to learn from her that hard work is good and right and necessary; that the happiest moments in life are those of simple sharing and love; that debt is to be avoided; that there is such a thing as right and wrong; that we are members of a nation with a particular history and it behooves us to know about it; that music and storytelling are gifts to be thankful for; and so are the stars over the prairie, and plum trees in blossom, and the ability of men to work in perfect rhythm to construct a railroad. I want to take the best of the Little House lifestyle and use those ideas to help create a warm, loving, calm, cheerful, God-fearing atmosphere in my own home. I will use my computer, my VCR, my beloved washing machine, my hot running water, my gas oven, and my cell phone to help me do that. And I thank God many times a day for the modern technology that allows my husband and me to stay home full-time with our children!

Religion:
An Intimate Relationship with God

Good literature and a learning-all-the-time lifestyle can be the foundation of religious education as well as academic education. It works its way into the heart and soul of a child and works to change the child into what God wants him to be. Living biographies of the saints are powerful tools in educating our children. These books don't just touch their minds; they penetrate their hearts and burn an impression on their souls.

Of equal importance is the relationship that the student has to the teacher. Edith Stein did not speak much on home education, but she did talk about the role of the teacher and the role of the mother. By putting them together, we get a clear idea of the responsibility a home-educating mother has in the formation of her children.

First, Edith Stein sees a loving, nurturing relationship between teacher and student. She considered teaching a "religious calling" where "the teacher stands as a mediator between God and the student." The teacher is called to "open her student's soul to the workings of grace. Both the teacher's attachment to the student as well as the student's trusting devotion to the teacher are characterized by objective love. Such objective love draws the educator to the child. She wins the love of her pupils not for herself but to direct them to the…content of the curriculum." (Woman, 9)

When writing about the role of parents, she points out that "the ideal home is a place where the children grow up under the responsible care of both parents, in a circle of brothers and sisters, and in an environment adjusted to the physical and spiritual needs of the child and the adolescent. When this is so, the home will naturally transmit what we have come to regard as the formation of the person…a formation which is silent and persistent, which in part operates unconsciously in harmony with the natural laws of growing up and in part works consciously under the guiding and forming influence of the environment." (Woman, 221)

Edith Stein believed with her whole heart that faith and character are transmitted best through relationship. That is the foundation of the philosophy of education presented in this book. Children are formed by the relations they have with the people and the ideas in their lives. A child first learns holiness by watching his parents. That is an incentive for us all to grow in grace in our vocations as parents. We don't have to be perfect. God has designed it so that we can all learn and grow together. Being a teacher and mother is our path to heaven — it's through our vocation as mothers and teachers that we cultivate our child's heart and character so that they end up on the path with us.

Nowhere do we want our children to have a more intimate relationship with the subject at hand than in the teaching of the faith. "Religion" doesn't fit in a box in a teacher's plan book. It envelops every waking moment all day long (and some dreaming moments too). To live an authentic Christian life, the child must be aware that the Holy Spirit walks every step and breathes every breath with him. More than anything else, it is our witness that *shares* faith. It doesn't teach faith; faith can't be taught. It demonstrates faith; it invites faith. We endeavor not only to teach children the intellectual dimension of the catechism, but also to form them religiously. Edith Stein writes, "Thus we can also say that to be formed religiously one must have living faith. To have living faith means to know God, to love Him, to serve Him." (*Woman*, 138)

Like everything else we teach a child, the atmosphere and the discipline of religious formation is integral to its success. Catholics have rich traditions of the liturgical year upon which to build a foundation of both knowledge and love of God and his Church. It is in living the liturgical year with our children in the heart of our families that we are best able to convey the expression of genuine faith in the beauty of the Catholic Church.

Every family will live the liturgical year differently and much can be gained by the exchange of ideas. Entire books have been written on celebrating the Church year in the family. An investment in some of these books will serve you well as you plan to introduce the living ideas of the Church to your children.

Within the liturgical year is a precious rhythm of feasting and fasting, opportunities to experience again and again the Passion and the Resurrection. Indeed, there are also those opportunities within the Mass and within  the week. Where do we begin? We begin with a single day. The day should begin with prayer. Teach your children a morning offering and pray it with them. From the time they are small, encourage some quiet time in the morning to give the day to God. Consider making daily Mass part of your routine.

Each mealtime should begin with grace. The Angelus can be said at noon and the rosary after dinner. With a house full of wee ones, one can't expect perfect attention for an entire rosary. Try a decade. Use pictures to represent the mysteries. Let each child who is able take a turn leading. We have found the Children's Rosary tapes by Lion Communications to be invaluable. Simple daily prayer routines are reminders of God's omnipresence and channels of his grace.

Moving beyond the daily routine, a calendar is absolutely essential to planning your weeks, months, and years to embrace the Church. Each week, be mindful that Friday is a day of sacrifice and penance and Sunday is a feast. As a family, establish habits and traditions, that will become as natural as breathing to your children. For instance, on Sunday, we always go out for bagels after Mass, frequently joining Patrick's godfather and his wife. The children give us narrations of the homily over bagels and we all discuss it together. Sunday evening, we always have ice cream sundaes after dinner — "Sundaes on Sunday." Both rituals are simple and they set the day apart from the rest of the week.

The seasons of the Church year and the celebration of saints' feast days throughout the year are opportunities to grow as a family in a deeper understanding and appreciation of the faith. This will require some planning. I sit down, usually a season at a time — Advent, Christmas, Carnival, Lent, Easter, and Ordinary Time — and plan which saints to study and which activities to do. Some seasonal activities, like an advent wreath or a Lenten sacrifice crown of thorns, are repeated every year. Others vary with the year and the situation in our family. Some years, I do a lot of planning and activities; other years, I do much less.

Crafts, and reading and writing activities, are seamlessly incorporated into our lesson time, bringing home the point that there is nowhere that religion ends and real life begins. Particular Bible studies, meditations, saints' stories, and the celebration of sacrament anniversaries are planned for teatime. Teatime is my liturgical year tableau.

There is a pause in my life between the end of typical school hours and the busy rush of carpools to soccer practice that I have come to savor. In our house, we call it "Teatime." Every day at three-thirty, I put the water on to boil and call the children to set the table. The table is spread with a cloth reflecting the color of the priest's vestments that day at Mass: purple for Lent and Advent, white for feasts, green for Ordinary Time, red for martyr's feasts. We put classical music in the CD player, perhaps light a candle or two for the table, and enjoy some precious quiet time together.

A couple of years ago, if someone had told me that this scene would take place in my house, I would have been extremely skeptical. I had three very athletic boys, ages ten, six, and four, and a busy two-year-old girl. I put a great deal of thought into establishing this habit in our daily routine before I suggested it to my children. I knew I needed a time that would be sanctified, and I knew I wanted the routine to drive the celebration. I decided to begin the first day of school, but the first day of Advent, the first day of the New Year, or the first day back to Ordinary Time, would work equally well.

I stocked up on a wide assortment of fruit- and mint-flavored herbal teas (I did not want to caffeinate my guys at that hour of the day). Perusing cookbooks and favorite recipe cards, I planned for a week's worth of baked goodies, counting on having them hooked on this new family tradition by the end of the week. I also began to gather recipes from books like *The Continual Feast* by Evelyn Birge Vitz and *Catholic Traditions in Cooking* by Ann Ball. Some of these are dinnertime recipes and we use them then, but many are wonderful for teatime. The preparation is as much a part of the experience as the consumption, so the children are involved from the crack of the first egg.

On the first day of our new routine, with the smell of sugar and spice cookies hanging in the air, we gathered at the table. We began with grace for the first day of school, taken from *Let's Say Grace* by Robert M. Hamma. Then we just talked about the day and the year to come. It was nothing formal, but I was amazed at how calm everyone was, how I held their attention and they held mine, and how much we were enjoying this time.

After the first week, I further refined my concept. We always begin with grace, and Hamma's book has suggestions for holy days and feast days, keeping us effortlessly in step with the liturgical year. Then we do a brief fifteen-minute Bible study. I like using *Our 24 Family Ways*, published by Whole Heart Ministries as my guide. It is a Protestant publication, but since it is just a guide, I can easily adapt it to suit my needs. Occasionally, I will read a saints' story book, particularly if it is a feast day of someone I want to highlight. I also use the readings from that day's Mass. After Bible study, we usually just talk, although sometimes the boys will insist on a few pages from whatever chapter book we are currently reading aloud as a family.

During Lent and Advent, I have enjoyed using calendars of readings and meditations designed for families. I also spend a great deal of time gleaning wonderful ideas from *The Catholic Parent Book of Feasts* by Michaelann Martin et al., and *The Year and Our Children* by Mary Reed Newland. Both books could be very overwhelming if one were to attempt to do it all, but if we look at them as resources for discovering our own traditions, they are gold mines.

  The teatime ritual creates closure in our day and it gives us a "holy space" to bring some peace into our domestic church. Before instituting teatime, we would just slide from our relatively insulated "homeschooling" time into the rest of a daily life in the community. Even though we are certainly always learning, it's nice to have time set aside to tie up loose ends. The rest and reflection before plunging headlong into the busy afternoon does us all good.

  I have noticed that after the cookies are gone and the children begin to excuse themselves and leave the dining room, it is the child who has something on his heart or who simply didn't get much of my time that day who stays to linger over a second cup of tea and some time with Mommy. These are times I cherish.

  There is something about the inherent elegance of teatime that makes instruction in manners simpler than it is at dinnertime. I think my children sometimes imagine themselves to be British nobility or children of colonial Williamsburg. Setting the table and cleaning up is also simpler than at dinnertime and so inspires a spirit of genuine cheerful cooperation.

  An unexpected benefit of teatime has been the ease with which I can now incorporate special celebrations into our day. If it is a feast day or a baptism anniversary for one of my children, we invite their godparents to tea. The honored child chooses the food to be served. We set the table with a tablecloth, flowers, candles, and the good china. I don't worry about breakage because the atmosphere slows the children down enough that they are gentle. Handling fine things seems to quiet ordinarily active children. If someone were to break a cup, however, I would consider the experience of tea with real china worth the cost. Those dishes were rarely used until we established this tradition, and I relish the idea of my children enjoying them and storing fond memories of them during their growing years.

Usually, I will choose two additional saints per month to "honor" at teatime, along with any saints associated with name days. We will read about the saint beforehand and then brainstorm together on an appropriate food or drink or decoration to bring to the teatime celebration. Occasionally, we will invite a guest who might have a connection to the saint.

Teatime has opened a window on the joy of hospitality for my children. They are learning to set a table, to arrange the food attractively, and most importantly, to welcome people into our home to share our time. They are learning to be gracious hosts and gracious guests. Sometimes, this is a casual happenstance — a neighbor needs me to watch her son for an hour or so after school or a favorite uncle drops by on his way to an evening job and they join us for tea. We carry on with the plan, often exposing the guest to a lovely Catholic tradition. Other times are carefully planned.

Times of hospitality have offered my skeptical extended family a peek at our home-education atmosphere. They see that the children are learning well and they hear lively, intelligent conversation. It is a witness to the gentleness and grace of this lifestyle. In the first month after we instituted teatime, we celebrated three birthdays. Two of the celebrations were for children. We simply invited a few neighborhood children and the cousins to come over after school, decorated a cake, and played some games when tea was finished. The parties were simple, but the children were pleased. Patrick, my then four-year-old, even requested a special teacup as his most desired birthday present. Incidentally, it is also Patrick who is most precise about brewing his tea for exactly three minutes and never drinking it from a mug used for milk or juice, much preferring a proper cup and saucer!

The third birthday celebration was for Grandma. The boys helped with all the preparations from setting the table to picking the flowers to baking the cake. Grandma was truly touched by her elegant party and duly impressed that it had been catered by her usually rowdy crew of grandsons.

Another unexpected benefit of our afternoon repast is that we are all less likely to fall victim to the five o'clock crankiness so easily attributed to low blood sugar. A planned snack at three-thirty is a very good thing. After about two weeks of this afternoon tradition, however, I noticed teatime being reflected on the bathroom scales. Now that I had them hooked with the help of sweet treats, it was time to add other snacks to our teatime repertoire.

I remember reading the advice to create "Sabbath Moments" in all our daystime to rest and rejuvenate our souls. Teatime does this for me and I am grateful for the opportunity to engrave the habit on my children's hearts as well.

Celebrating the liturgical year is an excellent opportunity for learning across the curriculum. Reading, writing, art, and music all have their place in the celebration of God's seasons. An example of an integrated lifestyle unit for Advent is included at the end of this chapter to inspire you to look at your "school" time a little differently.

Nature opportunities abound as well. Plant a Mary garden. Research all the flowers traditionally used to honor the Blessed Mother. Ann Ball's book *Catholic Traditions in the Garden* is a wonderful place to glean ideas to make your own.

What about formal religious instruction? It is necessary that children learn the doctrine of their religion. Memorization is simply a beginning — not an end in itself. It facilitates but does not substitute for real learning. Learning is integrating the facts into their hearts and souls. It is in living charity that a child learns charity. It is in experiencing forgiveness that he understands forgiveness. We can present the facts to a child in an orderly manner, using the *Catechism of the Catholic Church* as our teacher's manual and all the referenced scripture and doctrinal readings as our living books. We must educate ourselves to educate our children. We need to impart the very necessary philosophical book knowledge without boring the child to tears and abstracting it from real life and we need to touch the heart without resorting to the fluffy feel-good stuff that Charlotte Mason would call twaddle.

Edith Stein reminds us: "This cannot be done through tedious intellectual instruction, but it also cannot be done through fanatic instruction which 'appeals to the emotions'; on the contrary this can be done only through a religious instruction which leads from the fullness of one's own religious life to the depths of the Godhead, an instruction which is able to present God in his kindness; such instruction enkindles love and exacts proof through deed, and it may so challenge because one achieves this by oneself. Wherever the soul is enkindled, that soul itself longs for action; and it eagerly grasps the forms of practical life for which God and Holy Church have provided..." (*Woman*, 138–139)

Present the Catechism in your own words, commenting from your own heart. Then ask a narration of your child. As a family, go slowly through the sacraments, prayer, the Apostle's Creed, and the Ten Commandments as they are presented in the Catechism. If you are uncomfortable without a child's book at first, use the beautiful series by Inos Biffi. Be sure that the children are narrating after a small portion is presented. Use those narrations to make a notebook that will have far more meaning than a fill-in-the-blank workbook. Encourage the child to embellish the notebook with drawings and holy cards of saints that you study and celebrate at teatime. You will cycle through the Catechism several times as your children grow and they will come to the same information with increasing sensitivity and maturity. By the time they leave home, it will be their own.

We have found a wonderful resource for bringing religion to life in the context of a real story. Ignatius Press publishes a book that is a study guide to the Vision books biographies of the saints for nine- to fourteen-year-olds. The book, entitled *Saints of the Church: A Teacher's Guide to the Vision Books*, is a gem. I don't usually like study guides, but this one, with the books, could easily be an entire curriculum, save math! For each of seventeen books, the author provides an overview of the saint's life, vocabulary related to and referenced to the story, "language in context" (a list of quotes from the book that are perfect for copy work), a timeline, a list of geographical sites from the saint's life, and a lengthy list of report topics which the child or the child and parent together can research and narrate. There are also biographical sketches of other historical figures of the time that will inspire families to digress a little down some rabbit trails, revealing even more history. After the biographical sketches, the author, Michael G. Allen, provides a list of references to scripture and the new Catechism on different topics presented in the book. This list is ripe with opportunities for family discussions. Finally are the obligatory "class discussion questions." I think of them as conversation starters, not test questions.

A collection of the narrations following research on report topics, map work, copy work, and narrations on the catechism research would make quite an impressive religion notebook. My children are inspired by the biographies, and the inspiration gives rise to thoughtful questions and meaty discussion. I encourage you to read the books aloud to the entire family instead of assigning them as personal reading. Each child will take from the reading experience that for which he is ready. I am reading the books aloud to all my children and they really do hold the interest all the way down to my four-year-old. As much as I am able, I tie the reading to the liturgical year by introducing the story of the saint during the month of that saint's feast day.

In addition to reading inspiring stories, play liturgical music and celebrate the seasons in song. Collect art that reflects the faith. When exploring art, don't limit yourself only to the masters of classical art. Consider eastern icons, stained glass and architecture. All these media are expressions of faith. When your children are inspired to create their own works of art, encourage them to imitate the masters and to find fresh craft ideas. Ann Ball's *Catholic Traditions in Crafts* should get you started.

As your children mature and apologetics become a natural interest, introduce them to the wonderful tapes available on Catholicism. Listen together and discuss, discuss, discuss. I have found Matthew Pinto's book, *Did Adam and Eve Have Belly Buttons?* and Mary Beth Bonacci's *We're on a Mission From God,* to be great resources for engaging my older child in thoughtful conversations. I look forward to reading encyclicals together and to discussing a wide variety of classical theological philosophy from G.K. Chesterton to C.S. Lewis to Scott Hahn. Catholic television can also be a source of wholesome information. A child who is in his late elementary years will benefit tremendously from a regular confessor and spiritual director. No child should leave home to be an adult Catholic without reading one of the best examples of living books published in modern history. *Witness to Hope* by George Weigel is an excellent biography of Pope John Paul II. It is also a living world-history book, a living church-history book, and a living theology book.

It is also crucial not to forget that we are to know, love, and *serve* God. Even children can serve Him by serving others. It is heartwarming to see the effect that a baby in a front pack has on a roomful of senior citizens. It is lovely to watch a three-year-old present bread she helped make as part of a dinner for a neighbor with a newborn. It is encouraging to hear an impassioned seven-year-old explain his Precious Feet pin while he collects for a crisis pregnancy center. This is how children learn to live their faith. They walk with Jesus in a world that desperately needs living Christians. They are Christ to one another and to the world.

Linda McDonough relates:

> *I was reading **A Simple Path**, a book about Mother Teresa, and felt guilty. How could I be like her? The logistics and safety issues of taking my family into the inner city to help the poor on a regular basis overwhelmed me. "Lord, what do you want me to do? How can I develop a heart for the poor in my children?" And then it hit me. The essence of Mother Teresa's ministry was to give dignity to the dying. This is what my husband did as a Eucharistic minister. We began to make his visits to the shut-ins a family affair. We all join him for the first stop and then my youngest and I linger for a visit with this very special (and lonely) woman while my husband takes the older children to visit the rest of our people. We also try to incorporate extra visits and have added these special people to our prayer list.*
>
> *My husband and I often wonder who is doing the blessing. We have been deeply touched by these patient, long-suffering people who have a special love and concern for us. We have watched our children develop a tender heart for these frail people and learned that God can use them to minister to the suffering and dying. To see a child gently, but confidently hug a deformed body and to see the love between the two is to see Christ's love in a very special way.*

Above all, I want my children to be intimate with Our Lord. My husband and I endeavor to teach them those relationship skills they need for a mature intimacy. We teach them the catechism; we show them how God has revealed Himself to us in the Bible; we participate with them in the sacraments. And we pray. We pray with them — both spontaneously and from memory. We let them see us praying. We talk about prayer and offer prayer intentions as a family. When a big decision has to be made or big event is anticipated, we bring it before the Lord in prayer. When we are simply grateful for a day lived well, we come to Him in thanksgiving. We pray unceasingly. And we reiterate how God works through prayer. Living in such an environment, the children grow in understanding that praying isn't wishing upon a star but a dialogue with the Lord whereupon He transforms their souls. Prayer is an intimate friendship.

When we walk with the Lord and live in His light and our children walk beside us, they too are in the Light. It is our daily living, the rhythm of our lives, which will leave the indelible mark on their souls. We teach our religion when we live the faith. It is that simple. And it is not simple at all. It's a mystery. How very Catholic....

An Integrated Literature Unit for Advent and Christmas

The following is an example of how to make living the liturgical year all you do for "school" for a season. This is an Advent and Christmas unit. It was designed with the real limitations and demands of a large family in mind. It is not necessary to do everything. It is necessary to prayerfully discern what would best benefit your family.

One of my favorite children's authors is Tomie de Paola. A Catholic of Irish-Italian descent, he is not afraid to wear his faith on his sleeve. He liberally sprinkles references to Mass, the saints, and even confession throughout basically secular books that can easily be found on public library shelves. In addition to many folktales from varied cultures, he has also written several well-researched, beautifully illustrated stories of saints. And he has enough Advent and Christmas books to carry a family from the first Sunday in Advent through Epiphany.

In *Merry Christmas, Strega Nona*, many children will recognize dear old "Grandma Witch," who begins preparing for her traditional Christmas Eve feast on the first Sunday of Advent. She staunchly refuses to use the magic she employs during the rest of the year, insisting that Christmas has a magic of its own. Big Anthony, her bumbling helper, has a Christmas surprise planned for the old lady, and the entire town turns out to help him make the holiday a special one for her.

Next in line is *Country Angel Christmas*. I introduced this one on the Feast of Saint Nicholas, December 6. There is definitely a sense of Advent as a time of preparation as all the angels in heaven are preparing for the celestial Christmas celebration. The littlest angels are told to be scarce while the barn angels ready the animals for the procession, the kitchen angels bake, and the music angels rehearse carols. It is Saint Nicholas, in heaven where he belongs, who finds the littlest angels the all-important job of providing light for the celebration. This book works beautifully at the beginning of the season because, like *Merry Christmas, Strega Nona*, there is great emphasis on the preparation.

December 12 is the feast of the Lady of Guadelupe, and de Paola has an exquisite picture book by that name. The author is both a gifted artist and a superb storyteller. This is the story of the Aztec peasant Juan Diego, who sees Our Lady as a pregnant

Mexican woman and hears her tell him to build a shrine in her honor. He must convince a skeptical bishop. Mary graciously provides a miraculous sign, captured beautifully in de Paola's pictures.

Hispanic parishes always have a large picture of Our Lady of Guadelupe and carry it in procession on her feast day. True to his love of detail, de Paola depicts such a procession in *The Legend of the Poinsettia*. Lucida is a little girl who is helping her mother weave a blanket for the Christmas crèche at church. When her mother suddenly falls seriously ill, the child tries to finish the blanket herself. She tangles it miserably and is bereft at the thought of having nothing to bring to the manger. An old woman mysteriously appears outside the church and suggests she carry a bundle of weeds inside. The picture of Lucida kneeling by the crèche, surrounded by glorious poinsettias, is guaranteed to inspire you to run out and buy many, many of these flowers to adorn your mangers at home. Both this book and *The Lady of Guadelupe* are available in Spanish.

Closer to Christmas, *The Clown of God* is a lovely way to remind children that the greatest gift, indeed Christ's own gift, is the gift of self. A traveling juggler has spent his whole life making people laugh. Near the end of his days, he searches for the perfect present for Mary and the Infant. He learns and teaches a valuable lesson in giving.

Following the clown theme, *Jingle, the Christmas Clown* is an award-winner not to be missed. Jingle is the youngest clown in the circus, and the circus is traveling to the big city for its annual Christmas performance. Every year, the circus stops in a little village for Christmas Eve. This year, they arrive to find the village destitute. All of the young people have left; even the church is closed. The circus presses on, except for Jingle, the youngest clown, and the baby animals, who are too tired to travel. The little animals and Jingle put on a very special show for the old villagers. An angel appears amidst golden stars at the show's finale. The recipe for golden star cookies at the end of the book is a natural invitation to an afternoon of cookie baking and decorating.

On January first, *Mary, the Mother of Jesus* is a logical choice. This book is lovely and quite different from the author's typical children's storybook or his saints' stories. Mary's life is depicted in fifteen beautifully illustrated segments. In his forward, Tomie de Paola writes, "When I was an art student in 1956, I saw the Giotto frescoes of the life of Mary in the Arena Chapel in Padua, Italy. I knew that some day, I would attempt my own visual version of Mary's life. I have drawn on scripture, legend, and tradition for the praise of Mary, the mother of Jesus."

Stretching beyond Christmas Day and on to Epiphany, *The Story of the Three Wise Kings* recounts the legend of the Wise Men. They travel to Bethlehem to pay homage to Jesus. Along the way, they encounter Herod, and before their return, they are warned by an angel to travel a different route.

Finally, *The Legend of Old Befana* must be told. Old Befana is a cranky old Italian woman who is too set in her ways to get up immediately to follow the Wise Men, who are following the star to visit the Baby King. Because she sets out too late, she never catches up with the Wise Men's traveling party and so she searches still, leaving goodies outside the doors of children on the Feast of the Three Kings. "For, after all," says Old Befana, "I never know which child might be the Baby King of Bethlehem." Sounds like the beginning of a new tradition in our house.

Another very valuable resource is *Hark! A Christmas Sampler* by Jane Yolen and illustrated by Tomie de Paola. It is an anthology of Christmas legends, histories and songs that is wonderful for shedding light on many legends of today and yesterday.

Some of the activities listed on the following pages can be done by children alone, freeing Mom and Dad to do the myriad of tasks necessary to prepare for Christmas. Other activities are wonderful opportunities to share both quality literature and truths of the Faith as a family.

Activities for Families:

Week One: *Merry Christmas, Strega Nona and The Country Angel Christmas*

1. Make a list of all the Advent activities your family does. Compare the list with another family. Are there any new traditions you would like to adopt?
2. Write a family advent prayer. Pray that this will be a special time to prepare for Jesus' birthday.
3. Make puppets to dramatize *Merry Christmas, Strega Nona*. Perform the show for family and friends on Christmas Day.
4. Compare an icon of Saint Nicholas with de Paola's drawing in *Country Angel Christmas*. Draw your own picture of Saint Nicholas in any style you wish.
5. Make apple star prints. Cut an apple in half width-wise (surprise! there is a star inside) and use tempera to print the stars on paper. Or print them on canvas bags and give them as a Christmas gift.
6. Make glitter-glue stars to hang on the Christmas tree. Draw stars in glue on wax paper. Sprinkle with glitter. When the glue dries, peel away the wax paper. Use gold thread to hang.
7. The country angels harnessed a star to shed light on the Christmas celebration. During Advent, we await Christ, who is the Light of the World. Make an Advent meditation candle to remind you throughout the season that it is Christ's light that is a "light unto my path and a lamp unto my feet" (Psalm 119: 105). Decorate a large pillar candle with colored beeswax cut into figures which represent Biblical events from the time of Adam and Eve until Jesus' birth (supplies are available from Hearthsong 1-800-325-2502).
8. Make pasta. (Do you have a magic pot like Strega Nona's?)
9. Bake something that requires "peeling, sifting, pouring, and stirring" like the kitchen angels did.
10. Discuss the real hierarchy of angels.
11. Make a traditional Italian Christmas Eve dinner. Throughout Italy, traditional dinners include twelve courses, in honor of the twelve apostles. (See recipe box for ideas, including Big Anthony's cod.)

Week Two: ***The Legend of the Poinsettia and The Lady of Guadalupe***

1. Read about Christmas plants in *Hark! A Christmas Sampler* (beginning on page 60).
2. Read about Mexico. Find it on the map and tell about the country today. How is Christmas celebrated there?
3. Make Holiday Flan (See the recipe box).
4. The story of Our Lady of Guadelupe is presented as a legend in the book. Using another source, read about the Church's official teaching on Saint Juan Diego.
5. The crèche is an important part of the Legend of the Poinsettia. Where did the tradition of the manger scene begin? Read about it in *Francis, the Poor Man of Assisi,* by Tomie de Paola.
6. Make tissue-paper flowers in red, white, and pink, traditional poinsettia colors.
7. Copy de Paola's picture of Our Lady of Guadalupe onto cardstock using magic markers. Send it as a Christmas card.
8. Make a large banner of Our Lady like the one in the book using felt.
9. Have a procession like the one in the book. Gather up some friends to parade with you, and have hot chocolate and cookies afterward.
10. Make a manger scene using old-fashioned clothespins, doll head beads and felt (all supplies are readily available in craft stores).

Week Three (this will actually extend two weeks into Christmas week): *Jingle, The Christmas Clown and Clown of God*

1. Read the "Gift of the Littlest Shepherd" in *Hark! A Christmas Sampler*. Compare the gift of the shepherd with the gift of the juggler.
2. Make a gift coupon for each person in your family. Decorate them in Tomie de Paola's style.
3. Make a gingerbread stable for Jingle's animals. Use animal crackers in your scene.
4. Jingle took good care of the animals. Animals were also important to Saint Francis. Read "The Legend of the Birds" in *Hark! A Christmas Sampler*. Make a present for the birds using pinecones, peanut butter, and birdseed. Hang it with a Christmas ribbon on a tree in your yard.
5. Saint John Bosco could juggle. Find out how this skill was helpful in his ministry.
6. Learn to juggle.
7. Make star cookies using the recipe in *Jingle, The Christmas Clown*.
8. On December 28, the Feast of the Holy Innocents, read "The Dough and the Child" in *Hark! A Christmas Sampler*. Make yeast bread.
9. We tend to romanticize the stable. Take a trip to a working barn during Christmas week. Be prepared for unpleasant sights and smells. Imagine a tiny infant there.

Week Four: *Mary, the Mother of Jesus*
1. Read the book as a family and study the pictures. Compare the events depicted in the book with the mysteries of the rosary.
2. Illustrate the mysteries of the rosary, reflecting the style in de Paola's book. Use the illustrations for meditation when you pray the family rosary this year.
3. Also read *The Donkey's Dream* by Barbara Helen Berger.
4. Read and memorize "The Donkey's Song" in *Hark! A Christmas Sampler.*
5. Using a new calendar, write in all the Marian feast days and decorate those squares.
6. On January 1, we honor Mary in her role as the Mother of God. Choose a mother (or grandmother or godmother) you know who reminds you of the Blessed Mother. Write about it. Illustrate your essay with a border of forget-me-nots like those in *The Donkey's Dream.* Present your essay as a gift to the mother you chose.
7. Read "The Legend of the Rosemary" in *Hark! A Christmas Sampler.*
8. Make rosemary botanical candles. Wrap and knot a length of wick around a pencil. Suspend it across the top of a clean quart-size milk carton (cut the top off the carton to make it square). Melt beeswax in a clean aluminum can set in a pot of simmering water. Pour into the carton, filling the carton about one quarter of the way full. Let harden slightly and sprinkle with dried rosemary. Add more hot wax, to the halfway mark and repeat with the rosemary until you have filled the candle. Let harden completely (overnight). Peel away the milk carton.
9. Make Rosemary Chicken for dinner (See recipe box).

Week Five: *The Legend of Old Befana and The Three Wise Kings*
1. Read "The Littlest Camel" in *Hark! A Christmas Sampler.*
2. Read "Baboushka" in *Hark! A Christmas Sampler.*
3. On January 6, leave a little gift at a neighbor's door with a note signed "Old Befana." Keep the secret forever.
4. Make cardboard crowns. Decorate throughout January with one plastic jewel for every Bible verse memorized.
5. Make stars from translucent paper to hang in the window to remind you to always follow the star. (Hearthsong has kits for this 1-800-325-2502.)
6. Make King cake with little treasures baked into it. Serve with wassail punch.

Recipe Box

Flan

- 4 eggs
- 2 1/2 cups milk
- 1/2 cup honey
- 1 teaspoon vanilla
- 1 to 2 tablespoons warmed honey or syrup

In a medium bowl, beat the eggs until foamy. In a small saucepan, heat the milk and honey together just to simmering, and then add the vanilla.

In a slow, thin stream, beat the milk mixture into the eggs. Pour the mixture into a buttered 9" layer cake pan or flan pan. Place in a large, shallow pan or baking dish filled with hot water to a depth of 1/2 inch. Bake at 325 degrees for 35 to 40 minutes, or until the center is fairly firm. Glaze with the honey.

Makes 6 servings

(From *Joy to the World* by Phyllis Vos Wezeman and Jude Dennis Fournier)

Rosemary Chicken

- 2 pounds boneless, skinless chicken breasts
- 2 cans cream of mushroom soup
- 1/2 cup white wine
- 1 teaspoon dried rosemary

Flour the chicken breasts and brown quickly in a skillet with olive oil (no need to cook through). Put chicken in a Crock-Pot and cover with the rest of the ingredients. Cook on low 8 to 10 hours. Serve over egg noodles.

Italian Christmas Eve Dinners

Baccala alla Marinara

1/4 cup green onion, chopped	1/4 cup olive oil
3 tablespoons parsley, minced	1 cup tomato sauce
3 tablespoons basil, minced	2 cups dried codfish, shredded
1/4 cup mushrooms, sliced	Salt and pepper to taste

Soak the dried fish 5 days in plenty of cold water, changing the water twice daily. Do this outside the house because of the odor.

Sauté the onion, parsley, sweet basil, and mushrooms in olive oil until delicate brown. Add the tomato sauce and drained fish; simmer 1/2 hour. Salt and pepper to taste. Serve with polenta or cooked spaghetti.

From *Favorite Italian Recipes*
by the Saint Theresa Guild of Holy Rosary Church, Bridgeport, CT

Baked Stuffed Calamari

3 pounds squid, cleaned	1 teaspoon salt
1 clove crushed garlic	Freshly ground pepper
2 tablespoons parsley	1/2 cup dry white wine
1 cup fresh breadcrumbs	
1/2 cup oil	

Cut tentacles from squid: chop up very fine. Put into bowl and add the garlic, parsley, breadcrumbs, oil, salt, and pepper; mix thoroughly. Stuff squid with mixture and secure with toothpicks. Oil baking dish and line squid in it. Pour oil on top and add the wine. Bake at 375 for 50 minutes. You may also add 1 cup cooked tomatoes before baking.

Serves 6 to 8 people.

From *Favorite Italian Recipes*
by the Saint Theresa Guild of Holy Rosary Church, Bridgeport, CT

One of the great specialties of many areas of Italy is the "mixed fry." The *gran fritto misto* typically includes all manner of deep-fried foods, including meat. On Christmas Eve, there will be no meat, but rather different kinds of fish, perhaps some vegetables as well — and maybe even some fresh fruit.

Gran Fritto Misto "mixed fry"

Mixed Fried Fish, Vegetables, and Fruits. You can use any combination of the following:

Seafood: Smelt, codfish, fresh tuna, whitefish, salmon, fillet of sole, halibut, small fish balls, baby eel, oysters, shrimp, scallops. Fish should be cleaned and cut into bite-size pieces.

Vegetables: Zucchini, mushrooms, eggplant (sprinkle slices with salt and let sit for 20 minutes; wipe dry); partly cooked cauliflower or brocolli florets; artichoke hearts. Cut the raw or partly cooked vegetables into bite-size pieces.

Fruits: Apple slices, pear slices, strawberries, cherries

Batter (See recipe card for Fritto Misto Batter)

Vegetable oil for deep-fat frying

Heat the oil to about 370 degrees on a deep-frying thermometer.

Coat the foods completely with the batter and fry them a few at a time, turning once or twice, until they are golden on all sides. Do the fruit first, then the vegetables, then the seafood. Drain thoroughly on paper towels. Remove cooked pieces to a hot dish while you cook the rest.

Arrange everything attractively on a hot platter. Serve hot with mayonnaise or lemon quarters. Sprinkle fruit with granulated sugar.

From: *A Continual Feast* by Evelyn Birge Vitz

Fritto Misto Batter

1 1/2 cups flour	1/4 cup dry white wine or water
1/2 teaspoon salt	or 2 to 4 tablespoons brandy if frying fruit only
3 tablespoons olive oil	1 cup cold water
2 eggs, separated	

Optional: a little freshly grated nutmeg. If frying only fish and vegetables, add up to 1 teaspoon each of crumbled basil and rosemary leaves to the batter; if only fruit, add 1 tablespoon sugar.

Mix the flour with the salt. Stir in the olive oil and the egg yolks, mixing well, then the wine and water. Let the mixture stand for 1 to 2 hours.

Just before you are going to prepare the Frito Misto, beat the egg whites until stiff but not dry. Fold them gently into the batter. They do not need to be thoroughly incorporated.

From: *A Continual Feast* by Evelyn Birge Vitz

Creativity — Cultivating Color and Cacophony

A long time ago, someone told me that no one is really creative. Because God is the only Creator, we cannot possibly be creative. I can't remember where or when I heard this, but I remember its message well. It is a message that is simply not entirely true.

God is the Creator. "God created man in His own image, in the image of God He created him; male and female, He created them." He created us in His image! Because we bear His image, we reflect His creativity. We are like Him, though we are tainted by sin. We are all innately creative. We reflect His glory in our creativity. In his 1999 letter to artists, Pope John Paul II writes, "With loving regard, the divine Artist passes on to the human artist a spark of his own surpassing wisdom, calling him to share in this creative power."

Creativity must be nurtured to grow. Parents who educate their children at home often comment on how much they learn alongside their children. It is perhaps in the area of creativity that we are given the most license. As we age, most adults lose the creative drive. It is all but snuffed out by the noise and confusion of daily life. We begin to think that creativity is only for the professional artists, poets, and musicians among us.

John Michael Talbot, a popular Catholic musician, writes, "Unfortunately, many people don't necessarily think of themselves as creative beings. In part, that's due to churches that tell people to live according to strict rules of conduct, parents who snuff out their children's creative urges by telling them to grow up and get real, and schools that focus on producing graduates who can make a practical living instead of 'daydreaming' or 'fantasizing' about being artists" (*The Lessons of St. Francis*, 94).

Ironically, in the corporate world, creativity is what sets the successes apart from the rest of the pack. Management consultants call creativity "the ability to think outside the box." I consider creativity to be a necessity in homemaking. Are you serving boiled hot dogs on paper plates tonight or will you grill fish, steam vegetables, and bake bread to be served by candlelight? In the business world or at home, we are daily offered countless opportunities to create.

Typically, we think of inspiration followed by creativity. While it is certainly true that an inspiration may fuel an impulse, true creative work requires discipline. Certainly, these are what we desire for our children (and ourselves): the ability to listen to inspiration and the discipline to answer the call. Creativity is a whisper from within begging to burst forth. Children are blessed with abundant whispers. It is the noble duty of the parent educator to protect the creative impulse and to nurture it. At the same time, it is beneficial for the parent to quiet herself long enough to hear her own whispers and to discover alongside her child the joy of creativity.

The parent educator must equip her child to answer the call of inspiration. There are certain tools which are necessary for creative expression. Stock your house with crayons, markers, paint, and lots and lots of paper. Make them accessible. A neighbor once clicked her tongue as she examined the hieroglyphics of my four-year-old, saying, "My children were never allowed to touch the markers." Poor children. What dull lives they must have led! My children are invited to bring color into their lives. If that requires an occasional lesson on appropriate places to draw, so be it. The environment must support the artist.

Painting and drawing are not the only creative media. Don't stop with drawing and painting. Clay is essential in a creative home and it has the benefit of keeping busy hands happy while Mom reads aloud. Blocks are a creative medium. We have plain wooden blocks, castle blocks, architect blocks, and LEGO blocks of all sizes. Nine colleges recently moved to include LEGO blocks in their admission evaluation system. They will ask applicants to try to build a robotic Lego structure as part of their application. These schools are looking for students who think creatively.

Encourage drama. Dress-up clothes, flannel boards, puppets and puppet theaters encourage children to employ their imaginations. As children get older, scripts must be written and musical scores drafted in order to really produce a play. Around our house, plays are likely to become videos. We have discovered that video is a very creative medium.

There are children's theater opportunities in most medium to large communities. Seek out these opportunities if the child is so inclined. Children's theater can be a wonderful opportunity for an entire family to be involved in a substantial artistic project. The more it becomes a family project, the more it benefits parents and children alike. My experience has taught me to be very involved when one's child is a member of a children's theater cast. The long hours necessary for rehearsal should not be unsupervised hours. If the parent is involved, the experience can be a very beneficial and highly educational one for the entire family.

There are creative outlets in the garage, in the sewing room, and in the kitchen. It has been useful to me to try to think of our afternoons as time for creative endeavors. I plan for art activities and nature walks (which usually end in sketching and painting) in the afternoon. My children are fortunate to have a grandfather who will undertake carpentry projects and a godfather who happens to like robotic LEGO models. Both have been happy to spend an occasional afternoon engaged in a project with my children.

To encourage creative expression, we carefully plan for creative appreciation. I place a high priority on art and music appreciation. Children are inspired by works of great artists and musicians. To give them an opportunity to gain a familiarity at a young age is to give them a priceless gift. I have found that appreciation invariably spills over into the desire to create.

Charlotte Mason has greatly influenced my approach to art appreciation. She wrote: "The study of pictures should not be left to chance, but they should take one artist after another, term by term, and study quietly some half-dozen reproductions of his work in the course of a term…We cannot measure the influence that one or another artist has upon the child's sense of beauty, upon his power of seeing, as in a picture, the common sight of life; he is enriched more than we know in having really looked at even a single picture." (*Home Education*, 306)

We study one artist every six weeks, one print per week. I usually select the prints (usually 11 x 14 size) from the National Gallery of Art website because we live close enough to the National Gallery of Art to make a trip when our study is complete. I order prints online (it's about ten dollars every six weeks), allowing whoever happens to be around to help me choose from the online prints available to be ordered from National Gallery of Art's gift shop. Usually, there is a brief overview of the piece also online which I copy to my word-processing program and print for my own use and my eleven-year-old-son's notebook. I also grant one child the privilege of choosing the screensaver print for each week from what is available by that artist online. The child who chooses must e-mail daddy to explain what we did to his computer!

On Monday morning, we all look at the first print together. We study it silently for a few minutes, and then I turn it over. Beginning with the youngest, everyone must make an observation and no observation may be repeated. I turn it back over and offer them a little history about the artist and the print.

Then I invite the children to copy the print. I do not require this activity, but my eleven-year-old always does it gleefully and the others, seven, five, and three, usually give it a try. The children work on their prints, listening to classical music, for about a half hour while I get the rest of the week organized. Michael, the eldest, is never finished by this time but is usually ready for a break. We go on with the rest of our studies and he returns to finish his project when he desires. When everyone is finished copying, I put the print on the wall near the reading corner of our "learning room." Prints from past studies are hanging on the walls of the staircase, where quite a gallery is evolving. All of the children's drawings are stored in a portfolio, but I am going to frame a few of them. At the end of the year, I put all the prints in a binder.

On Friday of each week, I ask for an oral or written narration. The nice thing about verbally narrating something visual is that it stretches the child to employ descriptive language. These narrations are great opportunities to exercise creative writing muscles.

Some time during the course of our six-week study, we all attempt the activity for that artist suggested in *Discovering Great Artists: Hands-On Art for Children in the Styles of the Great Masters* by Maryann F. Kohl. The book suggests a hands-on art activity for each of more than seventy-five artists. With each activity is a brief biography of the artist and clear directions for the activity. The book is geared for elementary-aged children, but I have wanted to do each project along with my children, and the projects are certainly challenging enough for teenagers.

When we finish our six-week study, we go visit the prints "in person" at the National Gallery of Art. My father loves art and either takes the older boys and leaves me home (which makes me very sad) or comes along so that I can manage my small crowd in downtown Washington, D.C. Special visiting exhibits are set aside in the museum, and audio tours are available. The children are given the opportunity to listen as they desire (when they are older, I think I will require it). There is a small gift shop dedicated to the visiting exhibit and when we are finished, I allow them to purchase a small treat there. I don't demand a narration after these trips, but that is exactly what comes spilling out the moment they see Daddy or Grandma, who ask about their visit!

I know these field trips won't be available for every artist we study, but one of my goals is for my children to be intimately acquainted with the National Gallery of Art before they finish their schooling at home.

Occasionally, we diverge from the masters and study a children's illustrator in depth. We have done this with great success, using pictures by Eric Carle, Tomie de Paola, and Beatrix Potter. Each of these artists also offers literary opportunities. Eric Carle books are wonderful for introducing the study of insects. With *You Can Make a Collage*, published by Klutz Press, in hand, children will be thrilled to created masterpieces that look strikingly like Carle's work. Beatrix Potter was a naturalist in her own right who lived in the Lake District of England when Charlotte Mason did. She is a certain inspiration to nature journals. And Tomie de Paola's books explore ethnic and Catholic themes with style. Not to be missed is *The Art Lesson*, in which de Paola makes a not-so-subtle commentary on school art lessons that will bring back childhood memories for most parents.

Whenever we read a picture book, we spend some time looking carefully at the drawings, and the children often choose to copy illustrations. The children typically pursue this activity on their own, during leisurely afternoons.

As they have indicated an interest, I have investigated drawing textbooks and programs. The best I can recommend is *Draw and Paint Today*, a comprehensive multi-media program in drawing and painting instruction that really yields impressive results. I wouldn't attempt to use this or any program before the child is ten years old, though. Until then, let the child experiment, offering guidance or suggestions only if they are solicited and offering praise effusively.

Music appreciation follows a similar pattern. I choose one composer every six weeks. We read a little about his life and listen to a *Music Masters* cassette which intersperses his music with an interesting biography. Once a week, we repeat the cassette. Then, we play the music often — very often — for the next six weeks. At the end of the six-week period, the children offer narrations of the composer's life. Often they will also hum their favorite musical passages as well. There are some terrific Microsoft computer programs that will take you through a reading of the score, so you can listen, see the score, and read historical and musical commentary. We have Beethoven's Symphony No. 9 and Vivaldi's: The Four Seasons in this format. We study the artists as we get to learn a piece.

 Make music more than just background noise. Sit the children down occasionally and practicing really listening. Choose both vocal and instrumental pieces for listening practice. Michael Card is a contemporary Christian artist whose lyrics are as lovely as his distinctive music. He is easily understood by children, but his work is rich in artistry. Michael Card is an excellent place to begin to listen seriously together.

Thus, music appreciation is not limited to the masters. Indeed, we enjoy listening to Celtic music, contemporary Christian music, folk music, popular children's music, and even the occasional pop music (very carefully screened). Our home is rarely quiet. I believe that music has the capacity to transport a soul from despair to the light. Authentic, artful Christian music is priceless. In Patrick Madrid's *Surprised by Truth*, Julie Swenson, a convert from Fundamentalism, writes about the way she was moved after listening to John Michael Talbot: "The more I listened, the more I suspected he did know Christ in a way I did not. He wasn't merely singing about Christ, he seemed to be singing to Christ — to be worshipping him in song."

Edith Stein's biographer, Freda Mary Oben, writes of such an effect that music had on young Edith. During a time in her young adulthood which Edith termed her atheism, "she had just read a novel painting in most frightening colors the link between student alcoholism and amorality. She reacted violently. Nauseated, she lost her trust in humanity and was submerged under a pain of cosmic weight. It is an early instance of her concept of co-responsibility which we find developed to perfection in her adulthood." Stein was cured, Oben writes "…by attending a concert of Bach (whom she calls her 'Leibling' — that is 'darling' or 'favorite') where Luther's hymn, 'A Mighty Fortress is our God' was also sung…Her cosmic pain fell away." Shortly after this event, Edith was at last able to believe in a personal God. Music has a sure and distinct power over people. It is our duty and our privilege as parent educators to ensure that our children understand and appreciate this power and so use the tool accordingly.

Surely children are to be encouraged to create music as well as to appreciate it. The world cries out for holy art. John Paul II writes, "In order to communicate the message entrusted to her by Christ, the Church needs art. Art must make perceptible, and as far as possible attractive, the world of the spirit, of the invisible, of God. It must therefore translate into meaningful terms that which is in itself ineffable. Art has the unique capacity to take one or other facet of the message and translate it into colors, shapes and sounds which nourish the intuition of those who look or listen. It does so without emptying the message itself of its transcendent value and its aura of mystery." ("Letter to Artists")

Encourage your children both to create and to appreciate the kind of art about which the Holy Father writes. When the inevitable poorly chosen music or dramatic presentation begs for your child's attention, reflect together on the Pope's words. Teach children to be discriminating by giving them a taste for the very best. They will learn to judge well, and they will be inspired to create well.

Formal music training can take on many forms. All children should have some exposure to music theory and certainly to a broad knowledge of genres and instruments. When listening to a symphony in the car, play "guess the instrument," and soon the three-year-old can tell one instrument from another. You can also use the "Lester Family" a capella tapes in the car to develop an ear for harmony. Some children will be so inspired by great composers and compositions that they will yearn for more training and instruction.

As with so much in a living education, music training is a personal journey, highly dependent upon both the interest and aptitudes of the child and the circumstances of the family. With prayer, consider the child and the resources and then set about to plan a course of study. If a teacher is employed, do not relinquish your role as primary educator; rather, view the teacher as your accomplice and work together to acquire the finest music education possible.

Instruments, like art supplies, should be accessible. If your child can only get out his instrument when you get it for him, it will hinder his creativity. Do your babies like to bang on pots and pans? Just as you visit art, take your children to concerts. I think that we have a real advantage over families in Charlotte Mason's time in that we have both live and recorded music. Just as you study an artist, then see his work at a gallery, so one might listen to several classical pieces and then bring the children to a live perform- ance. This can be expensive, but there are free concerts and recitals at colleges throughout the country. The real trick is getting the children to listen at the concert — really not a difficult feat if the children have become familiar with the pieces before they attend. Call the public relations office for the performers, or check on a website for information.

Children's concerts are also a possibility, but they can sometimes be full of screaming children who don't really want to be there. This is not a pleasant experience, nor is it good for one's children to see. Consider a special day with mom or dad — perhaps a dinner and a "grown-up" concert — and the experience will be memorable. My children have all been to concerts since (before) birth, and are usually well behaved. When they are familiar with the pieces, though, it is a joyful experience for all. Their eyes light up, they draw in their breath, and sit at the front of their chairs! "We know this piece!"

Dance is unique in art education because it also provides physical education. Little ones love to move to music, and the transition to more formal dance lessons is usually an easy one. Just be sure to choose instructors carefully. The world of dance, like the world of theater, can be one which fails to support those values we hold dear. Watch to ensure that modesty in dress and movement is evident in a studio and its performances. Take particular care to listen and watch for the subtle or not so subtle jabs at body image. We want healthy dancers who praise Him in the dance. There is nothing lovelier than a roomful of little girls in skirted pink leotards gracefully moving to lovely classical music.

Art education is not an extracurricular pursuit. It is as integral to a child's education as art itself is integral to the expression of man's soul. We need beauty to be fully human. It is in art that the Holy Spirit breathes. The Holy Father writes, "Every genuine inspiration…contains some tremor of the 'breath' with which the Creator Spirit suffused the work of creation from the very beginning. Overseeing the mysterious laws governing the universe, the divine breath of the Creator Spirit reaches out to human genius and stirs its creative power. He touches it with a kind of inner illumination which brings together the sense of the good and beautiful, and he awakens energies for mind and heart which enable it to conceive an idea and give it form in a work of art. It is right then to speak, even if only analogically, of "moments of grace" because the human being is able to experience in some way the Absolute who is utterly beyond." ("Letter to Artists")

In the learning home, a day in which art has been appreciated and even created is a day on which we can all retire at night and utter, "It is very good."

Words from the Wise

How do you nurture creativity in your home?

Kim Devers, Kentucky

I constantly review materials in the evening hours. We invest in many materials, too many to accomplish in a lifetime. Having so many good resources available could become overwhelming, so I make time to plan a new activity often. In this manner, I express my creativity. When I take the time to plan an activity, like making candles or dough crosses, it allows for a really relaxed atmosphere the next day. Such activities create an excitement and joyfulness in our school. Naturally, creativity flows in a stimulating and relaxed atmosphere, especially at home. I try also to go along with ideas while gently steering the children to accomplish the task at hand. For instance, adding a little personal touch to a project is encouraged, but doing a completely different project during the activity is discouraged.

Trisha Artigues, Mississippi

On a good day the TV is not turned on at all. This is the single biggest contributor toward my children playing creatively. Worlds are created, animals come to life, toads are caught, pictures painted, stories created, all because they are left to their resources for entertainment.

Cutting back on out-of-the-house activities also ensures plenty of time for creativity to bloom. This is an aspect of Charlotte Mason's philosophy that I embrace totally; children need loads of time to play, to create, to discover their world.

Finally, I believe that through narration creativity is allowed to blossom. The child is able to choose his own words to express what he found to be important about a given book or experience vs. filling in the blanks to complete our ideas of what is important on this topic.

Creativity is one of those intangibles, really. We think we want our child to accomplish specific things in a given year and creativity doesn't fit nicely into any subject area specifically. It is something that, like most things, develops over time usually by what we don't do vs. what we do! If we can get out of the way and quit making our children fit into someone else's mold of what they should be and let them develop into the child God created them to be that creativity flows. This is not to say that we aren't there for gentle guidance, just that we stop scheduling away all their time and let them be children.

Cindy Kelly, Texas

I think the three primary ways we keep creativity flowing in our house is to provide the fuel, and fan the flames of creativity, and restrict TV and other forms of "screen time" which we find douse those creative flames very quickly! The fuel is primarily provided by living books. We find it is vital and we try to have a great read-aloud going all the time, plus lots of other fiction and nonfiction books available. I encourage my boys to read alone, but we still do read-alouds. Nonfiction books, including Dorling Kindersley or similar reference books are really fun to read through together, just picking out what we like and talking about it.

I also scan catalogs, science and toy stores, and garage sales, for finds to keep on my shelves. There are many science experiment books and kits, art and craft ideas and other things that can give great fuel for creativity. If I have them on my shelf waiting, an opportune moment can be pounced upon! I find that if I can give them a steady diet of new ideas, I will see the ideas resurface in their games or in connections they made to other "subjects." If the ideas wane, boredom grows and creativity dwindles.

Fanning the flames can be fun, if I will block out time with my children often and spend time exploring with them and helping them to make connections. I remember when I worked in corporate America; a management seminar I attended once explained that the primary job of a supervisor was to help their employees get their jobs done, through greasing the wheels, providing the materials or helping them sort out a difficulty. On our best days, that is my role with my boys. We have time, and I am not distracted or on a "schedule." We can read or explore together or they can alone. When they get stuck, or want to find a shovel to further pursue some nature study, I'm there to facilitate. I may offer guidance on how to find things in reference materials or suggest ideas on where to look next. Those days are wonderful, because their creativity is flowing and boredom with studies is far away.

We cut down drastically on TV and have very limited computer time and I have found a direct relationship between how creative my sons are and how little screen time they have. I am convinced it douses a child's ability to think and be creative when they watch massive amounts of TV, or play too many computer and video games. Plus it is so much fun to see them "discover" a great book, talk about the characters, play them out in life, and relate them to other facets of their lives. They are really, really thinking!

Describe your art program.

Cindy Kelly, Texas

When I first was looking into Charlotte Mason, I was immediately drawn to the art, music, and nature, because to me, they were things I always wanted to do myself but never really had the chance. I was so excited to finally have the opportunity to learn about art in a nonthreatening environment. I had taken a required art history course in school (snooze...) and had volunteered to teach an art appreciation course to my son's class when he was in public kindergarten (canned). Now, we could do things our way! I looked at all the study guides I could find and some of Charlotte Mason's original writings and very quickly came up with a program for art that we have continued, on and off, for the past three years. This is one of the few things that has not changed much since I brought my boys home.

First, I find an artist who is of interest to myself and my boys. I usually get prints from either the National Gallery of Art (www.nga.org) or from calendars at bookstores. I always use prints that are 11 x 14 as it is much easier for the children to see the details than with smaller prints. I will collect four or more prints (for Monet we had about a dozen) and hide them in the house well. Once I have some prints, I make a trip to the library and get some books on the artist. I always look for a Mike Venezia book on the artist (great children's books that talk about artists in a very funny and nonthreatening way), then I will throw it on the couch and let the guys "discover" it. Also, I will pick up some other children's books on the artist (which usually just get skimmed through) and a "coffee-table" book of their prints. I don't let that one out until the end. I will read most of the children's books and some of the coffee-table book to get a general overview of the artist. I also look for cues for the artist's worldview, so I will be prepared to bring that into the discussion, but that is often difficult to find presented in a balanced way.

Then, the fun. We usually do art study once a week, for however many weeks as I have found prints, one print per week. It is always on the couch, sometimes with a full blown "tea," or sometimes with just cookies and cocoa. But it is always a treat, always positive, and never a chore. I only allow them to look at one print a week. And I must say, I have been forcibly assaulted by my youngsters trying to get to the rest of the prints! (That is why I hide them.) We eat and talk and look at the print. We pass it around. Everyone has an opinion, even if it is "I don't like it — it is dark!" Even two-year-olds have an opinion! I will gently point out some things I have read about the artist — how he uses his brush, that he loved nature, why he liked to paint in that region — as the conversation lags. If it doesn't lag, I try to keep quiet (which I must admit, can be difficult for me).

After our discussion is played out, the boys run off and I take the print and put it into a pretty gilt frame I bought at the craft store. I hang it on a prominent spot on the wall about four feet from the ground where the boys will see it every day. It will soon become a familiar friend. Next to the print, I mount an 8 x 11 sheet of paper that has the artist's name, important dates and regions and five or six pertinent facts about him. I try to include a humorous or controversial fact or two. I print it in a nice font and put a background colored mat behind it, and try to make it attractive. I include whatever I have learned, and know that I have probably missed the important parts, but just do my best! I leave it up for the duration of the art study. Each week we will bring out another print, and after we study it, it will get the place of honor in the frame, and the previous print(s) will be hidden until the end of the study.

After we have looked at all the prints, and hopefully had some good talks, I either tape all the prints on the wall, or we just place them all on the floor to compare. We will rate our favorites, discuss the "worst" and remember the past few weeks. When we studied Monet, we had all twelve on the wall at the end of the study! We left them up for two weeks! A regular gallery! One afternoon, my eight-year-old son sat on the couch and looked over at the wall and pointed out what a striking contrast there was between the detail of the painting — some were blurry and surreal, but others were very clear. I had not noticed that until he pointed it out. Pretty great!

We have been very informal in our art study. We have actually studied perhaps five artists in the past three years, as we have many moves and a scattered schedule. But, my boys and I have become acquainted with Monet, Rockwell, Rembrandt, Homer, and Picasso. When the boys walk into a museum and see a Monet they are very excited that they "know" him. The artist is theirs. Maybe I have only given them five, but that is five more artists than were given to me.

Another wonderful aspect of art study is the invitation it gives us to discuss worldviews: ours and other's. Picasso gave us some great discussions. Why was he so angry? Why the total turnarounds in his style? I had to censor many of his prints, but my boys saw much of his style. How could a person have such drastic changes of feeling and heart? What must his life have been like? Did faith play any role in anchoring his life?

When we studied Monet, my oldest son was mesmerized as Monet loved nature as my son does. It showed in his paintings and was mirrored in the biographies he read and I paraphrased for him. But then one author wrote how Monet painted furiously at the end of his life as his eyesight was failing him. He loved nature and its beauty so much — more than anything else — that he had to get it all down on canvas. My son's question was, "Did he love nature more than God?" We wrestled with the concept. He had a hard time looking at Monet after that, and has had to reconcile that for himself. That has given us a bounty of discussion points.

Although art study has been an on and off endeavor for us, primarily due to time constraints, it has been exceedingly rewarding. It is a time of closeness, of nonexpectation between myself and my children, and a nonjudgmental time of looking at the world, others' interpretation of it, and expressing our thoughts. It is a fertile ground to bring in the ideas of others and discover how they can fit into our world and worldview. My heartfelt suggestion to those not familiar with art study is to read a bit of the ideas of Charlotte Mason, choose an artist, find a few prints, and jump in. Make it fun, nonthreatening, and relaxed. Just strive to give your children an introduction, a very slight one, enjoy discovering the artist with them, and later in life they might remember the artist as an old friend.

Can you suggest a good program for teaching music theory?

MacBeth Derham, New York

Suzuki music places a very strong emphasis on the parent as participant, not just onlooker. The parent is not only in the room during the lesson, but is encouraged to study the instrument along with the child. This helps the child see that music is important to the parent, and that everyone must struggle.

Most children quickly outpace the parent. Some people complain that Suzuki doesn't put enough emphasis on theory and reading music. This is true, so you must either get into a program that includes ear training and theory, or you do it yourself. I have had to occasionally supplement our local program with some old elementary music books (Silver Burdett, circa 1920) I found at a library book sale. In a time when all elementary teachers could play the piano, these books were used to teach sight-reading and ear-training. Loki Music has a beautiful Catholic sight-singing course with tapes that we have used to supplement as well.

What are your favorite resources for sharing music with your children?

Susanne Kain, Michigan

We had a wonderful classical radio station that was replaced by something less than favorable. This gave us our first leisurely introduction to a wide variety of classical music at home and in the car. From there we discovered **The Classical Kids Series** *which my children still beg for and will listen to intently. Then, we purchased the* **Music Masters Series** *which we will start this year. Another resource we have from my dear mother-in-law is* **100 Masterpieces: The Top 10 of Classical Music**. *This ten-volume CD set ranges from 1685–1928 with each CD spanning about fifty years. As the composers are various on each CD rather than one composer it can give a real feel for what the era was like and how it correlates to the happenings of that particular time. Some books include* **Lives of the Musicians,** *which has nice short biographies with information that "neighbors never knew," and* **The Spiritual Lives of the Great Composers**. *We also have fun with a nice keyboard my son received for his birthday. We create different tunes changing the beat, rhythm, pitch, and tone. There are numerous styles of music and we'll take one of those, get an ear for it and dance away, clapping and tapping.*

Is it necessary to be musical to teach music appreciation?

Susanne Kain, Michigan

I hope not. My best friend growing up was/is a wonderful pianist. She would spend patient hours teaching me songs to play through memorization and ear. That and my tiny Magnus Organ with chord keys and my S&H green stamps guitar with self-taught chords was my extent. I did grow up with music playing a lot of the time. While it wasn't classical it was diverse and it was pretty hard to grow up in Motown and not be able to "hear the beat." I do agree though that there's an additional appreciation for music if you understand the difficulty in creating that music. I learned that to a certain degree by sitting next to my pal for hours on end looking at all those lines and lines of notes and watching her fingers fly around on the keys. It amazed me....I guess what I am trying to say is I believe you can be musical without knowing how to formally play an instrument.

Why should dance instruction be a part of my children's education?

Missy Gurley, Virginia

But why should they dance? Well, Scripture tells us that there is indeed "a time to dance" (Ecclesiastes 3:4), and exhorts us to "praise Him with the dance" (Psalm 150:4). Charlotte Mason encourages us to "give the child pleasure in light and easy motion" and that "the delight in the management of one's own body in dancing...should make part of every day's routine." She also sees "certain moral qualities in alert movements, eye to eye attention and prompt and intelligent replies," and cautions that, "often good children fail in these points for want of good physical training." Indeed we are body-soul composites and our temples and those of our children are surely not to be neglected. But why should they dance? Why not just jog around the block or do jumping jacks in order to nurture our physical nature?

Indeed, our dear Miss Mason lumps dancing in with drill, calisthenics, and even horseback riding. Yet, as a dance teacher and a home educator in the style of Miss Mason, I propose that we see dance well apart from these other physical endeavors. I propose that we dance for the same reason that we open living books to our children. We dance in celebration and affirmation of Beauty. We dance because, in the words of Pope John Paul II, "every genuine art form in its own way is a path to the inmost reality of man and of the world. It is therefore a wholly valid approach to the realm of faith, which gives human experience its ultimate meaning." Now, could this possibly apply to little girls in pink tutus, and even bigger ones dancing the **Nutcracker**? *Indeed! These ruffled beauties (and of course even men in tights!) can dance because the dance is meaningful in itself; the dance is a step outside the work-a-day world into the realm of the contemplation of Beauty. The Council Fathers of Vatican II explain that "the world in which we live needs beauty in order to not sink into despair." And Pope John Paul II tells us that; "Beauty is a key to mystery and a call to transcendence." And amazingly, when "'the beautiful' [is] wedded to 'the true' through art, souls might be lifted up from the world of the senses to eternal." Certainly these lofty, yet very real ideas apply to all art forms, but how in particular can all of this relate to little tutus?*

The prolific Catholic philosopher, Josef Pieper, in his book **Only the Lover Sings** *explores the world of recreation ("the liberal arts") in a way that will help us answer our dancing question. He explains that our time away from our work ("the servile arts") should not be spent only in preparation for the next day of work! Rather our recreation should truly be a re-creation. We are creatures of a Creator. We mirror the image in which we are made when we ourselves create. And "the divine Artist passes on to the human artist a spark of His own surpassing wisdom, calling him to share in His creative power." (John Paul II) The dancer in front of the mirror has been given another medium with which to mirror the Creator.*

This true re-creation is sought out not because of its "usefulness-for-something-else", but because it is "meaningful in itself." This brings up an essential point! If one dances because it is an activity which is meaningful in itself, not in order to make the cut for the New York City Ballet, then everyone can dance! Whatever the body type, natural ability, or level of coordination, let them dance! We dance not solely to make the company, we dance to contemplate truth and beauty and in doing so we mirror our Creator.

Pieper explains that "an activity which is meaningful in itself cannot be accomplished except with an attitude of receptive openness and attentive silence." Are these two notions not the soul mates of Mason's Power of Attention? A cooperative dancer in the hands of a reverent teacher stands at the barre in front of that mirror with the same receptive openness and attentive silence, all the while nurturing that power of attention that will affect the rest of her endeavors.

Our case for dance is certainly building, but Pieper offers a great caution. "Artistic activity especially can denigrate either into idle and empty game playing or into some novel and sophisticated form of business and nervous distraction — if it does not simply sink to the level of crass entertainment apt to seduce man to make him a prisoner of his workdays with no thought of escaping!" It seems that Pieper understands another key concept of Miss Mason: TWADDLE! As in anything, great prudence must be shown in choosing the teacher and the arena in which your child will seek out beauty, because the artist even on such a valiant quest may lose the way. Choose carefully that space, that studio that holds the barre at which your dancer will practice receptivity, and the mirror through which she will mirror the Creator.

Pieper notes a further elevation of recreation, the last in our analysis. Actively creating refreshes and sharpens our ability to see. The artist sees the world with a particular vigilance and "long before a creation is completed, the artist has gained for himself another more intimate achievement: a deeper and more receptive vision, a more intense awareness, a sharper and more discerning understanding, a more patient openness for all things quiet and inconspicuous, an eye for things previously overlooked." And from within the studio, at the barre and in those mirrors your dancer may perfect the art of narration without using any words at all.

Pope John Paul II explains that "in order to communicate the message entrusted to her by Christ, the Church needs art." He informs "the artist of the written and spoken word, of the theatre and music," that "creation awaits the revelation of the children of God through art and in art." I exhort you to raise up your children to effect a change in the world of the arts in our culture! Certainly there is barely a theatrical event that isn't an affront to truth and beauty. Our Holy Father has petitioned us, and our little ones, yes the ones in the tutus, at the barre, in front of the mirrors, at the studio may be just the ones to answer his call.

Special Blessings

There is a child in my life who delights in bringing me tiny treasures he has found — a perfectly shaped leaf, a dandelion, a shiny rock, a smooth stone. He notices the smallest details and shares them with me with a shy smile. It is this child who has taught me the most about mothering and about teaching; indeed, he has taught me the most about life itself. And I know the lessons are not nearly over.

When he was born six years ago, I regarded him as nothing less than a miracle, a sign that I was being granted a second chance at life. I had battled cancer the year before he was conceived, and my husband and I had been told we might never have another baby. Christian was the child born after cancer, the child whose birth heralded life.

His early days were quiet. He loved to nurse and to be held and carried. When he was in my arms, even strangers commented about what a contented baby he was. But as he grew, he was anything but contented.

Unhappy in anybody's arms but mine, in any other setting than home, he was a difficult child to get to know and an exhausting child to mother. Since my first son had been nothing like this one, I was plunged into doubt and despair. What was I doing wrong? Why was he so unhappy so often? How could I mediate in order to convey to other people how wonderful he was? Did I really believe he was wonderful?

My prayers were for patience and understanding. I wanted desperately to know what made this child tick and to know why life seemed so difficult for him. Christian hated to go shopping, to go visiting, to go to church. Anywhere that was likely to be crowded or strange was an obstacle to be avoided or overcome, not an adventure to be embraced. Birthday parties that delighted other children overwhelmed him. The bombardment of sensory experiences — songs, games, food, and sometimes the bright lights and animated characters of places designed to entertain children — were a personal hell for him. Either he would curl up into himself in a quiet corner or he would cry so violently we would have to leave.

We discovered that food sensitivities played a part in his inability to process stimuli. In addition to the real physical reaction (hives, flushes, and GI distress) he would get whenever he ate food containing artificial color, flavor, or preservatives or some foods containing naturally occurring salicylates (such as apples or cinnamon), he would have a neurological reaction. The neurotransmitters in his brain would "misfire."

But food was only a piece of the puzzle. Come with me for a moment inside his brain: It is a relatively quiet day. The toddler is napping, the three-year-old is still, and big brother is off in his room with a book. I am reading aloud to Christian and he knows that he will be expected to narrate after I finish. In the quiet of the kitchen, he hears the refrigerator buzzing. Just as he figures out the source of the noise and turns his attention to me, the ice machine begins to fill. This time he asks about the noise, interrupting me. I answer briefly and direct his attention back to the passage at hand. The morning sun is streaming across the table and he begins to feel warm. Simultaneously, his socks feel too tight, the seam is pressing unbearably across his toes, and the tag in his T-shirt itches. He takes off his shoes, still trying to listen. A truck roars by outside and the smell of diesel fuel wafts through the window. He is overwhelmed — sounds, sights, smells, and tactile overload. He dissolves into frustrated tears.

Some would say he needs a good spanking. But a sore bottom won't make the sensory interferences go away, nor will it teach him how to cope with what most people don't even notice. He needs a sympathetic, extremely patient parent who can allow him to be himself while teaching him how to get along in the world. He needs someone to understand that he marches to the beat of his own drummer and sometimes no one else can hear the drum. On good days I can be that parent; on bad days I fall pitifully short. The Charlotte Mason lifestyle does help tilt the scales in favor of the good.

It took me so long to understand that it was I who needed to grow and embrace this philosophy. I tried and tried to create the perfect learning environment. Ironically, I was a special-needs teacher before having children. And I tried to bring the perfect classroom home. But he didn't — and doesn't — need a classroom. He needed me to bring a gentle way of learning and understanding into his life. Probably more than most children do.

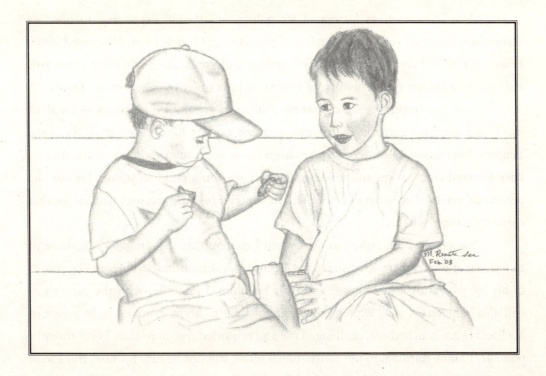

    The true fruit of my prayers for patience and understanding was the moment, real and palpable, when I suddenly understood that I needed to accept Christian as he is. Lying beside him in bed one night, repeating the tired ritual of lulling him to sleep, I found myself growing increasingly impatient. There was so much I needed to do and I felt like I was wasting time as Christian rubbed my upper arm in an effort to soothe himself and fall asleep. From out of nowhere (the Holy Spirit?), it dawned on me that there was nothing I could do about the fact that this tactile need was real for him. There was nothing I could do about the fact that he was more content if I met his need for my presence. To nurture this child and to educate him, I had to give until it hurt. I had to stretch.

    I couldn't change Christian's makeup. I couldn't make him into the child I had envisioned before he was born. I couldn't make him like noisy children's party centers. I couldn't keep him from cringing in a crowd or crying in church. I couldn't crawl inside his head and process information for him so that sights and sounds and textures would not be so overwhelming. And I couldn't make him act like my other children. I needed to acknowledge deep within my heart that he was God's creation, not mine. God has a plan for him. All I need to do is ensure that his education facilitates that plan.

Almost as soon as I stopped struggling and started expressing to him my acceptance, I noticed such exceptional qualities. And my love for him blossomed into a flower of rare and singular beauty. With greater understanding and sympathy towards my son came greater understanding of myself and the other members of my family.

I am also beginning to see that his challenges are also his blessings — for all of us. This little boy's extreme sensitivities — some experts have called it ADD, some Sensory Integration Disorder, but the diagnosis is really unimportant — sensitivities have fostered compassion and tenderness rarely seen in a child so young. He has the perceptual acuity of an artist or a poet, and he experiences both the pain and the joy that come with these gifts.

Sometimes I am moved to tears when I contemplate the struggles still ahead of him. Even at home, there are distractions aplenty. I pray that there will always be people in his life who truly know him — and truly love him. I pray that with the pain, there will also be poetry. I can't express how grateful I am to know him and to be a part of his life. He has touched me, challenged me and rewarded me more than I ever thought possible. I know learning, in the conventional sense, will not be easy for him. But I look forward to learning alongside him. And I am ever so grateful that we will be ambling together down the road that this gentle learning lifestyle has paved for us.

Words from the Wise
A conversation with Kim Devers, Kentucky

What factors would impede the success of a living-books education at home with a special needs child?

A mother giving too much authority to outside therapists, doctors, and other resources could really stifle the movement of the ever-changing Charlotte Mason homeschool environment. By other resources, I do also mean canned curriculums, even those geared to the child with special needs. Who's to say your child will have the same limitations another child with the very same diagnosis has? In fact, the experts these days would agree that every child is very different. How could a canned approach, even if developed by the best of minds, even begin to predict what your child is capable of doing at a certain age level, given the influence of his siblings, his social environment, his spiritual life, his interests, his overall development?

What factors will "guarantee" success?

A "living" program designed by the mother and/or father. The "schooling" must revolve around the interests of the children. A textbook/workbook approach could really bog a mother down — maybe even cause her to consider putting all the other children in a school away from home in order to "focus more on the child's emotional and educational needs." For example, if a mother's idea of moving from one level to another is centered on the idea of a child working his way through a stack of workbooks labeled "second grade level," then her focus will be on getting that child through those books. She would have to push aside the child's interests or "distractions" (which, we all know, sometimes lead to very real learning situations). And the mother may be battling against, instead of working with, the child's physical limitations. We all have limitations, especially physical ones.

One of the most important things for everyone in a home with such a child is to realize that the child may physically be unable or unready to accomplish a task that mentally he is capable of. For instance, take math. Say a child knows well and good that two plus two equals four, but he hasn't yet matured enough physically to be able to write without great difficulty. This is frustrating to such a chid who may know all the answers on a worksheet but cannot yet communicate by writing, and may not even be able to effectively communicate verbally. At this point I move away from therapists in my opinions. I believe that Mom and Dad, but especially the parent that works most of the time with the child knows the child's weaknesses and abilities better than any professional anywhere anytime. That being the case, only Mom can provide the very best education possible for that particular child. I've yet to meet a homeschooling mother who thinks she knows everything and never looks up information for her children. Nevertheless, I have met some mothers who think, or have let themselves believe, that others know what is best for her child. Therapists are simply another resource for the homeschooling mother; they are not God. Books are resources, but they are not the Word of God. God did not give your child to doctors, to therapists, to a school system, or to the government to raise. He gives the child to the exact parents that He handpicks. He will provide, so long as the parent is wise enough to use the resources available to her. He will provide the love, the patience, the endurance, the energy, and the right resources at the right times. We must have faith in God in dealing with a child with special needs, and we must have faith in our own abilities and talents.

How can a learning lifestyle benefit children with special needs?

Already in our home with a two-year-old who has Down Syndrome, we are very blessed with joy. By that, I mean we have come to love schooling. We enjoy the rhythm, the changes that happen over time, the interaction we have as a family, and the arts. The arts are such a benefit to children, who, in a way, all have special needs. Music is beautiful, so a frequent stream of classical music to ponder wakes up part of the brain that would otherwise "sit there." Looking at beautiful art puts lovely, lovely images into a person's brain, giving the person his own creative thoughts and ideas. Such thoughts transfer over into other subjects which may otherwise be thought of as "dry" (i.e., history, science, math, geography...). However, when the mother realizes the beauty of the Truth in all matters, these subjects tend to lose their dryness and come to life. All of a sudden, a family realizes that they love to learn about heroes, and the states and countries, and hey! We even like to learn the patterns in math!!! Such a way of living the Truths of knowledge instills a love of learning in the children. In answer to the question, there may be no "special needs" in some areas of learning, other than a special need of closeness with the teacher/Mom and the rest of the family, who already love learning and are full of joy.

What kinds of supplementation would it require?

Yes, there are times when help is needed. If a child needs glasses, he must go to a professional. If a child can't walk, he needs help from someone who has studied in such an area. When a mother doesn't know Latin, she must purchase a program or arrange for a tutor for her children. In the same way, if a child has special needs, say in speech, he may need outside intervention. A mother using Charlotte Mason must take the advice of others and pray, and then decide how to use such knowledge. The mother may even need to rethink her former way of disciplining a child. She may need to read books about alternatives to spanking, whereas spanking always worked with the other children. Maybe a child with difficulties in motor processing needs more "exercise" and the mother must use a few extra workbooks she didn't have to use with her older children. The mother can still use Charlotte Mason's style by having short, one-on-one sessions, giving much praise to her little child for accomplishing so much! Also, more hands-on-type materials may be necessary to keep the attention of such a child. I've had to add many new materials for my five-year-old daughter, who is a very independent learner, and totally different in her learning style than my oldest child (who does very well with more traditional approaches). Teaching in the home is a constant learning for the mother and the entire family. We must be guarded against being "set" in one way of thinking about schooling, in order to mature as a family seeking the way to God who gives us free will. We must allow our children with special needs to develop their own free will to desire good, while at the same time giving them the necessary tools for living pleasantly on this earth.

Sports: A School of Virtue

I married an athlete. I fell in love with a boy in a baseball uniform who grew into a man with a passion for athletics. My husband, Mike, was a student working in the athletic department of a large university when we got married. I have nursed babies at college sports camps, at professional soccer games, and on airplanes full of basketball players. My last three babies have taken their first steps in order to reach and kick a soccer ball held out to them. My current baby can't even walk yet but he can kick a ball across the room, scooting along on his bottom. It's little wonder that my children are all athletically inclined.

I have done much soul-searching on the role I want athletics to take in the education of my children. Athletics are vital to every child's development. Whether a child pursues a personal fitness activity like running or biking or a team sport like soccer or baseball, he or she must move. Our bodies are the temple of the Holy Spirit. They were designed to move, and they reflect the glory of the Creator in their movement. "In Him, we live and move and have our being." There is so much research on the benefit of exercise that its importance is irrefutable. Saint Thomas Aquinas wrote, "To a good bodily constitution corresponds the nobility of the soul." Aquinas considered taking care of the body a virtue. He asserted that after our minds and bodies are relaxed through exercise, we are better able to concentrate on philosophical pursuits. We must encourage our children to move!

Physical education is as integral to the formation of the character of a child, and later an adult, as art, music, or even academics. We are created to move, and since we are created in His image, that movement can and should bring us closer to Him. For children, organized sports are an excellent character-training tool. By this, I do not mean that I believe that coaches are training my child's character. Ideally, they do. But my experience has been that what a child does with sports in terms of character is up to his parents.

It is good for a child to learn to be a part of a team and to work toward a team goal. But character development in sports goes beyond the team and being nice and playing fair. It encompasses handling all the emotion that goes into gearing up for a big event and then needs to be channeled after a loss or a win. It involves striving for personal excellence and learning to accept one's limitations…and discerning where excellence meets limitations.

The Jesuits have seen this component historically, and the importance of athletics is evidenced in the biographies of people privileged to have old-fashioned Jesuit educations, from Babe Ruth to Pat Buchanan. Today, I think we can see this traditional emphasis on athletics in Legionaries of Christ, Opus Dei schools, and youth programs.

Athletic competition teaches resilience, a character trait that will be necessary as a child grows to face the many challenges in his life. No one wins all the time. How do we handle the losses? How do we want our children to handle the losses? There will be losses aplenty in life. Athletics afford the opportunity to teach children about them in a safe place.

When children are between five and ten, offer them opportunities to try many types of physical activity. The child who is fearless on the soccer field may cower in a martial arts studio. Conversely, the child who can't stand the pace of a soccer game may relish the discipline of karate. Some children will love everything they try. Then it is time to help them pare down and focus, if only because it is physically impossible to commit to too many teams simultaneously.

Consider your family situation as well. Will it work for someone to drive a child to the pool or ice arena early in the morning if they decide to pursue swimming or ice hockey? Is there one sport that really suits everyone and will streamline your activity a bit? For instance, some families find that swimming is ideal because all ages are at the pool at once. The bigger the family, the better. A wide age span with many children guarantees there will be someone from the family in almost every swimming event.

Some children may appear to have no natural aptitude for sports. It is important for them to at least be "athletically literate" just as we want art and music literacy. That is, the child should have the skills necessary to pursue personal fitness for a lifetime. Athletics take up time and energy that otherwise might be directed toward less wholesome activity. Pope Paul VI wrote, "Athletic commitment provides an effective antidote to the idleness, laxity, and soft living, which usually constitute the fertile ground of all sorts of vice." (February 28, 1978).

Pope John Paul II, known in his younger days as a skier and swimmer, has had much to say on the benefits of sports: In *Sport As Training Ground for Virtue and Instrument of Union Among People*, Rome, December 20, 1979, he writes:

> *The Church has always been interested in the question of sport, because she prizes everything that contributes constructively to the harmonious and complete development of man, body and soul. She encourages, therefore, what aims at educating, developing and strengthening the human body, in order that it may offer a better service for the attainment of personal maturation.*
>
> *Sport has, in itself, an important moral and educative significance: it is a training ground of virtue, a school of inner balance and outer control, an introduction to more true and lasting conquests.*

The Holy Father writes on the subject again in *Human and Sporting Qualities Make Men Brothers*, Rome, June 20, 1980:

> *Not only does the player find, on the level of the body, the relaxation that he needs, not only does he acquire additional suppleness, skill and endurance and strengthen his health, but he grows in energy and in the spirit of teamwork.*

And later in the same article he writes:

> *In the first place, sports make good use of the body, an effort to reaching optimum physical condition which brings marked consequences of psychological well-being.*

The Holy Father, also refers to the need for sports, nowadays especially, in the article *Be Examples of Human Virtue, Rome,* September 2, 1987.

> *Sport is also an important moment for guaranteeing the balance and total well-being of the person. In an age that has witnessed the ever-increasing development of various forms of automation, especially in the workplace, reducing the use of physical activity, many people feel the need to find appropriate forms of physical exercise that will help to restore a healthy balance of mind and body.*

There is a place in every curriculum for athletic development. Children need to learn personal fitness skills. Consider, too, equipping a child with social athletic skills like golf. There are usually community programs that teach children skills. For a child who is beginning later and may be shy about appearing awkward in front of his peers, consider some one-on-one instruction during the day when most children are in school.

Make athletics a family pursuit. Try hiking or biking together. Consider some less commonly pursued sports like water-skiing, dance, or racket sports. If you take the lead and find something you enjoy, your children will follow. When athletics become part of the family culture, they are infinitely rewarding.

There may come a time to help a child who appears to have an athletic gift to develop that gift. Just as we would nurture a musical or scientific gift, parent educators should consider athletic talent seriously. With any talent lies the responsibility for good stewardship. This is a challenge we strive to meet in our family.

When my eldest son, Michael, was two, the coach who brought Pelé to the United States watched him dribble a soccer ball down the hall at the university where my husband worked. "That child has incredible timing," he said. "What a gift and what a responsibility." That same coach sat with my husband, Mike, in his office watching the video of Michael's first game when he was six. Mike was watching on video because his job took him away that weekend. Michael scored seven goals that day. It was fun for us to watch him on the field, white-blond hair streaking hither and yon while he loved every minute of it.

The other parents got a huge kick out of it too…until the second game. Then he scored thirteen goals and it was sort of getting obnoxious. The coach was being pressured to rein him in. That's a tough call, too. How do you tell a six-year-old not to try? How do you tell him not to go after that ball when he has just spent the whole week dreaming of this game? This scenario repeated itself over and over until he was eight. That was the last season he played in a house league. The coach told my husband that he was glad to have Michael on the team because he (the coach) was learning so much from him.

This crossroads is where Michael's gift became our responsibility. We needed to help him to achieve personal excellence and to balance his life. We needed to understand that for Michael soccer was actually a way to bring glory to God — to express His hand in creation. Home education has been a blessing in this regard.

On the house teams, Michael was learning that he didn't have to try very hard to be the best player out there. He was learning that excellence (in terms of results) was easy. But he wasn't learning much about challenges or personal excellence. He was learning to be lazy. He also really wanted to improve his game. He was thirsty for good instruction. To get that, we needed to move into competitive leagues. This required more time, more travel, and more money. The return on the investment is excellent coaching, travel, experiences with other children who are similarly gifted, and countless teachable moments. Already, it has also been an almost weekly opportunity to witness, for us and for him.

Down the road, I see the same scenario with at least two more of my children. We will have to reevaluate where we live and where they play in order to create the best situation for everybody.

Our priorities and our gifts should determine how we spend our time. My husband is a television producer whose emphasis is on live sports. His schedule is rather unusual. He works odd hours and requires large blocks of creative time. I write a regular column and have been working on several book projects.

Our children seem to have inherited both a creative dimension and an athletic one. They love to write "books" and they inhale art supplies. There is a natural emphasis on creativity and athletics apparent in how we structure our time. Lots of uninterrupted creativity time is built into each of our schedules. This might be a key to our collective sanity.

The other key is physical activity. We have a state tae kwon do champion and four others on their way to black belt. Our first three children all play soccer and baseball, and the fourth dances. The other younger two were kicking with considerable accuracy before they were walking. My husband and I coach the younger teams. Our calendar in the spring and the fall is crafted with the precision of the technical engineers that we are not!

The time we spend in the car traveling to soccer fields is spent listening to classic books on tape and good music. These books have become part of our family's shared experience. The time spent on the field with a ball honestly feeds our souls. Over time, I have learned not to resent the afternoon rush to the field but to embrace it (including the commute). Like so many things about the home-education lifestyle, this is an ongoing process of dying to self and even sacrificing for the greater good.

It is true that we miss having dinner as a family frequently during the busy sports season. Because my husband often works at home, we are able to eat an unhurried meal in the middle of the day. If he is away from home during the day, we try to have unhurried discussion time at bedtime.

I also tailor my academics to take into consideration what is happening with the team. If Michael is in the midst of an intense practice period, we pull back a little on what is expected at the "school" table. We look at education as a year-round pursuit in order to make this work. I also know when to say when. My children all want to swim on the neighborhood swim team. It would be great fun and a good social situation. But I absolutely cannot do that after an intense spring and before an intense fall. There is temperance here.

Between their sports schedules and Mike's travel and home education, I have very little "Mom" time. I have to be very, very creative here, trading baby-sitting with a neighbor so that I can slip out and meet a friend for lunch, using e-mail as an outlet and a support, and promising myself the "reward" of late-night phone calls to far-flung friends where I know that I can shore myself up. And because I know that exercise affects how I think and feel very positively, I get myself out of bed before my little ones awaken to spend solitary time on a stationary bike with some good spiritual reading.

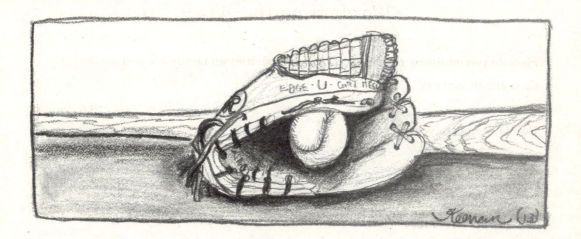

Because soccer is a team sport, I accept the fact that I need to work around the schoolchildren's and working moms' schedules. That also happens to be most coaches' schedules. Fortunately, soccer is usually played at really nice parks around northern Virginia. I find myself doing lots of nature study with my other children or just grabbing some playground time (something I find I do a lot less with my little ones now than I did when Michael was little).

We have made dear friends on the sidelines of soccer fields. They are woven into the tapestry of our lives. My husband and I have learned valuable lessons as well. For us, sports have been a window on the world, so to speak. As the children grow, we give them greater freedom in choosing teams and deciding upon a level of commitment. We encourage them to begin to shoulder the responsibility for their own improvement. We have also noticed that team sports are a valuable way for a child to begin to discern what he values in a friend.

Children who are educated at home generally do not share much of the popular culture with traditionally schooled children. They don't listen to the same music, watch the same television shows, or play the same trading-card games. The playing field becomes an opportunity to relate to other children. Home-educated children will need much guidance in this area. Our children are learning to be ambassadors for Christ, and sports are a universal language, bridging cultural as well as religious gaps.

Words from the Wise

How do you minimize the stress of outside activities on family life and maximize their enhancements?

Bob Davenport, New Mexico

I think we use outside activities to provide teaching and learning experiences in areas that would take a lot of energy and time for us to do on our own. I think doing this allows us to concentrate on teaching what we teach best. Thus, outside activities have become an intrinsic part of our homeschooling. As homeschoolers we have the ability to schedule outside activities throughout the day. However, we have found that it is important to protect large blocks of time (no outside activities) for our usual at-home work and play. Conversely, we try to schedule outside activities back-to-back or in groups to minimize wasted transportation time.

Also, we made a conscious choice to live near the center of town so our children could walk or bike to many of their activities. As to maximizing enhancement, I would say that if we choose to do an activity, we commit the time and effort to make it worthwhile. For example, our oldest son is on a swim team. If he did not practice regularly, we would drop swimming.

If your child is exceptionally gifted in an area, does this change your attitude toward an activity? (For example, if your son is a talented gymnast, are you more willing to pour time and money into that activity than for a son who is less talented?)

Bob Davenport, New Mexico

We would have a slightly different take on this. If the outside activity is exceptionally rewarding for the child (i.e., if we have a terrific piano teacher who our child is really learning from), then we tend to put more resources in terms of time and money into that activity. If an activity turns out to be only so-so, it gets pruned out pretty ruthlessly. There are too many other good uses of time (including a child's free time).

If your child isn't talented at all in an area, do you push to get him up to a functional level? (For example, if your daughter doesn't have an artistic bone in her body, do you spend time and effort in drawing lessons so she can have fun with a nature journal?)

A qualified yes. We are trying to educate well-rounded children who are not afraid of any appropriate physical or mental activity. So, when our son seemed overcautious and afraid of heights, we put him in gymnastics for a year or so. Once he was not afraid anymore, we dropped it. We didn't really care if he could do a cartwheel or not. We did care that he was afraid to try to do a cartwheel.

How do activities foster self-confidence, character, and love of learning in your child?

Most of our activities require practice. Our children (and I) are learning that how you practice actually counts more than the game, the race, or the recital. This translates directly to life, how you live day to day is more important than the crisis situations and really determines how one responds in crisis). This fosters self-confidence and character. Love of learning is fostered by exposure to a wide range of activities, usually at a higher level than we could provide. I think it is terrific when our children are coached or mentored by people who are successful in their chosen vocation.

How do you balance excellence in a particular area with being well-rounded?

We have a core of activities that get highest priority. These would be the activities, I suppose, in which we are seeking excellence. Other activities come and go, and are used more as exposure to a subject. Still, my oldest is only ten, and it would be unrealistic of me to state that we have solved the trade-off equation between excellence and rounding. My gut feeling is children should have the highest number of activities when young, and the activities should be pruned down as the children get older, with intensity in the remaining activities going up.

Is it necessary for every child to participate in competitive sports?

Linda McDonough, Arlington, Virginia

I've done a great deal of pondering over the role of athletics in the homeschool. Sports are very much a part of our family culture and something that we all enjoy. We have also found them invaluable for character formation, particularly in the areas of perseverance and self-control. I have found a range of homeschool philosophies when it comes to organized athletics. At one extreme are those who see sports as an encroachment on family life and secular teammates a corrupting influence. They often see competition as a negative and choose to avoid all forms of organized sports. On the other extreme are those families whose schedules revolve around afternoon sports schedules. This group sees sports as an essential component of the well-rounded person and believes that the ability to excel in a competitive environment will serve the child throughout his or her life. In between are all sorts of combinations including those who play on teams because their friends do it, because their parents want them to develop certain skills, or to simply burn off energy.

I am a big believer that every child needs to be developing lifelong fitness habits. Exercise is important to the proper functioning of the body. When our children go off to college or get their first desk job, we don't want them quickly adding an extra fifteen pounds. I also believe that children need certain minimal athletic skills which will allow them to play "pick up" sports with friends and not feel embarrassed or left out. This will also allow them to learn new sports as adults.

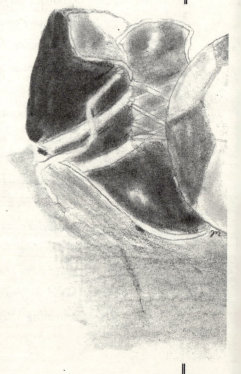

In observing and asking various families about their attitudes toward sports, I've concluded that there are as many ways to incorporate sports and activities into family life as there are families. It all starts with family culture. Some families love the outdoors. They would rather spend their weekends hiking, fishing, and camping than tied down to the weekend sports schedule. Others have children with special athletic talents which they feel God has called on them

to develop. Some families simply love sports. They play a different sport each season and make it a family affair with parents coaching or organizing teams. The key for both families and individual children is finding a team or activity which will provide a positive experience for your child.

Once your child reaches about eight or nine, finding the right fit can take some effort, but I believe it is essential. If (you or) your child is competitive or particularly gifted at a particular sport, it can be frustrating playing on a team where everyone else is there for social reasons. On the other hand, if your child is somewhat tentative about athletics, being on a team with friends can help him gain confidence. For many children, asking them to play in an intensely competitive situation is a sure way to turn them off to the sport for life. It is also important to consider your child's temperament and natural abilities. We had a couple of children on our predominately social soccer team who always lagged behind. Both those children turned out to be gifted swimmers. What is a disadvantage for one sport is often an advantage in another. My children come in extreme sizes. One is off-the-chart tall, another off-the-chart short and another is average height, but built like a tank. We're trying to channel each of them into activities where their body size is an advantage and something they feel good about.

Temperament also plays a large role in what a child will like. Some children thrive on a team; others prefer individual sports or lessons. Sometimes it's not the activity itself, but the coach that can make the difference. My pediatrician told me once "it often doesn't matter what, but who." Logistics can also play a major role in determining whether an activity is right for your family. An activity that is five minutes from home is much easier on Mom than one that is fifteen or twenty minutes away. Certain sports, such as swimming, work better for large families because often everyone can practice at the same time or are at least in the same meet. There are so many combinations, and often it is by trial and error that we find the best way for each child and for our family as a whole.

The Practical Side of Atmosphere
Children, Chores, and Character

When I was pregnant with my second son, despairing of how I'd ever keep the house clean with two little boys, a dear friend read the following quote to me: "Like the sun rising in the heights of the Lord, so is the beauty of a good wife in her well-ordered home." (Sirach 26:16). It is interesting that in the New American Bible, this verse reads "...a radiant home." My friend suggested that I meditate on it and that it would bring great peace when I was in labor and beyond. It took me awhile to figure out all that she meant.

I am a morning person. There is such promise and hope in a new day. I enjoy the quiet in the anticipation of the bustle to come. Morning is a respite, a pool of refreshment, and a time to focus. So, too is a well-ordered home. Radiance connotes warmth, brightness, and blessing. That's what I wanted for our home: both order and warmth. I didn't want a sterile house that wasn't cozy and inviting. On the other hand, I didn't find chaos and clutter warm or comforting. Can a home be both well-ordered and radiant? Definitely. We can bring warmth and peace and order to our homes so that they bring the peace of a beautiful sunrise to our families and ourselves.

Our homes are to be havens for our families, from our husbands right down to the littlest baby. We all experience a nesting instinct, which seems to inspire us to create a radiant home for our fulfillment. Homemaking involves a combination of physical labor and good management habits for us and for our children; but even more importantly, it requires self-discipline and great growth in virtue.

Conquering Clutter

I have wrestled with how to approach this topic. In my mind, people who are so bold as to write about it must have perfectly well-organized households. I have researched extensively and I try hard, but I beg you not to surprise me with an unexpected visit to check my competency in this area. Some days are better than others, and homemaking is a work in progress.

The journey to a clean, orderly home has been a long one. I did not come by this naturally. Cleaning was the first area I tackled, and devising a surface-cleaning scheme was relatively simple. Despite cleanliness, disorder and chaos were still part of our family life. I was usually frustrated and irritable at the state of our house. It was clean but it was cluttered. *Things* were taking over our life. Managing things, organizing them, cleaning them, picking them up, and putting them away was consuming my time at home. I began to talk to other homemakers about clutter.

I found that women are evenly divided on this issue. Either they will defend their right to accumulate and store things or they will absolutely declare war on "stuff." Depending on my mood, I agreed with one side's philosophy as often as the other's. I was worried that the anticlutter attitude was too rigid and controlling. But when I began to evaluate my own feelings toward my house, I recognized that clutter bothered me even more than dirt. If I came downstairs in the morning and faced a cluttered living room and a kitchen counter buried in children's papers and mail, I immediately felt disgruntled. I lost the peace of the sunrise.

If I began my day with a clean, clutter-free house, I was decidedly more cheerful. I had a sense of a day stretched invitingly before me instead of a day that had been sprung upon me. The ultimate question was whether a clean, clutter-free home would bring us all closer to heaven. A study of the lives of the saints answered with a resounding, "Yes!"

Clutter is composed of extra possessions which draw heavily upon the time and energy of the owner. It is possible to get to heaven under the heavy load of great material wealth, but it is undoubtedly a more difficult journey. Almost universally, the saints embraced poverty and simplicity in their lives. Saint Augustine wrote, "The love of worldly possessions is a sort of bird line, which entangles the soul, and prevents it from flying to God." Although I had approached the clutter issue from a housekeeping perspective, I came to understand it as a spiritual issue.

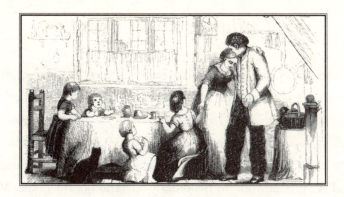

Consider this quote from *Upbringing* by James Stenson: "Being 'poor in spirit' (a Christian virtue) means being detached from things — being able to possess goods without being possessed by them. It means...putting people ahead of possessions — and seeing material things only as instruments for serving God and the needs of others."

Miki Hill, a frequent speaker at homeschooling conferences, advised me to look critically at my possessions and to weed out any inordinate attachments. During the second trimester of my third pregnancy, after I was past the tired, sick stage but before I was too big to move and in need of extra rest to prepare for labor and delivery, I went on an anticlutter crusade. I adhered by the strictest notion that if we hadn't used it in the past three months, we didn't need it. (I admit that this was a bit extreme but it felt great at the time.)

At this point, I had a choice: a garage sale or a charity. I opted for the latter because it was much easier to part with my possessions when I considered that someone might need them more. Saint John Chrysostom has said, "The man who owns two coats, not only should, but is obliged to pass one on to the man who has none." Furthermore, I was trying to practice contentedness with my state in life. Decluttering was a great exercise in stewardship and appreciation for the blessings we have. Saint Francis de Sales tells us that there are two ways to acquire all we want: keep getting more and more or desire less.

The anticlutter campaign raged in our house for almost a year. My husband and sons listened to so many anticluttering talks on tape as I researched that they also caught the bug. The children are learning that more isn't necessarily better; that they really don't need all the different action figures when one or two will do.

Children and Chores

Once the clutter was gone, I did a deep cleaning and put myself on a weekly cleaning schedule. It was time to train myself in the habit of orderliness before I endeavored to train my children. I read *Confessions of a Happily Organized Family* by Denise Schoefield and took her suggestions to heart. A deep-down cleaning, using her lists of what to clean, combined with disciplining myself in maintaining that level of cleanliness, laid the groundwork for the orderly operation of my home. My goal was to have everything ready before the third trimester so that I could focus on getting a good start on school habits before the baby was born. I knew that after the baby came, I wouldn't get to some of the heavy cleaning for quite awhile, but that a house freed of junk and cleaned thoroughly beforehand would withstand some benign neglect.

How did ordering my home help me create an atmosphere of education before and after the baby was born? There was a real sense of peace when I left a clean, orderly home to go to the hospital; I knew that I would return with a beautiful new baby and that his beauty would not seem out of place amidst the disorder. I planned for his homecoming as if he were a very important guest. The irony is that he's not a guest but someone who lives in my house. Shouldn't the people who live here be treated at least as well as company? It was also much simpler to resume the familiar routines my other children craved when the environment supported them.

A household management routine is crucial to a happy learning environment. Spend some time analyzing the components of your day in light of your responsibilities. The more tasks that can be done the same way at the same time daily, the fewer decisions and plans you will have to make. If you have never been especially organized or diligent, it is time to grow in discipline. It is also a good time to train your children in responsibility.

While we need to train children in good homemaking habits when they are young, we also need to strike the balance of excellence without expectations of perfection. When there are many young children home all day we have to accept the fact that at this stage of our lives, most of the housework is ours to do and our level of cleanliness will reflect that fact. Perhaps that is the toughest thing of all.

This area of homemaking is where not only Mom but also children have an opportunity to grow in virtue. Some of the most powerful character-training tools are in the broom closet. They are called mop, broom, and dust rag. Several studies, including one forty-year study done at Harvard, have proven that having household responsibilities as children is one of the strongest predictors of adult success.

When our society was more agrarian, children were integral to the survival of the family. Even school schedules were devised to enable children to be home at peak times on the farm. Now, children are largely a leisure class unto themselves and school breaks are clearly vacations. While that may seem to be progress, it can also be said that the lack of purposeful work in a child's life may be a cause of an increasing tendency toward many social ills including delinquency, adolescent depression, and suicide. Children have no sense of self-worth because they are not required to contribute to anything meaningful.

A young child who learns early that he is integral to the smooth operation of his home has the distinct advantage of feeling important beyond the "I'm special; you're special" hype promoted by Barney the dinosaur. The teenager rises above "Life's short. Play hard," advocated by Reebok. For children who build their self-esteem on nothing more than messages from popular culture, the inevitable questions are "Why am I special?" "Is there more to life than play?"

Children who are charged with household responsibilities reap the benefits of learning life skills, time management, and perseverance. If your children are trained in household routines from the time they are old enough to toddle, they will have a firm foundation of right habits upon which to rely. Over the long haul, children derive satisfaction at a job well done which goes far beyond canned warm fuzzies and carries them much farther into the real world than advertising hype ever will.

In *Upbringing*, Stenson notes that in large families delegation of responsibility seems to happen more naturally. Mom and Dad simply can't do it all. Families with several children either have well-organized home management systems where chores are delegated to all members, or very obvious chaos. Stenson comments upon how the growing trend toward smaller families and greater wealth has contributed to a distinct lack of purpose for children and offers words of encouragement to parents who are seeking to train responsible children.

In smaller families, there aren't as many tasks to perform, and they don't have nearly the magnitude. It's much simpler to cook and do laundry for four than it is to do the same tasks for eight. In families of greater wealth, everything from yard maintenance, to child care, to housecleaning can be hired out. Many children need to contribute nothing and indeed live an artificial life of leisure just before they are launched into the real world where life doesn't work that way. Needless to say, the world of work can be a shock to their systems.

When instituting a system of chores, the experts (parents whose children are doing chores and doing them well) maintain that the most important rule of thumb is to inspect what you expect. Teach a child how to do a task. Do it with him until you are satisfied that he knows it well, then check his work, every time, correcting if necessary. To require work and not ensure that it meets an acceptable level of workmanship is to encourage disobedience. By the same token, specific, honest praise is a necessary part of the system.

It helps to have a list from which chores are assigned. By listing the chores to be done each day and referring to the list when assigning tasks, the assignment seems less arbitrary. The child must do that chore because that is what is on the list, not because Mom or Dad is a dictator.

Another helpful technique we've discovered in our home is doing different tasks together in the same room on a rotating basis. When my six-year-old and I work together to clean a bathroom, he sees that I have a job too. He cannot claim to be the maid. He is part of a team. Close proximity makes it easier for me to correct mistakes and to praise instantly. Since we rotate the chores (every room gets a thorough cleaning once a week), I know that at least once a week I will have done everything necessary to keep things clean. With a very young helper, rotation has assured that while he is learning, the chores are still being done with adult efficiency.

Michele Quigley, a mother of eight children from Pennsylvania, suggests that for some children, it is useful to expect that chores be done before breakfast. "They are motivated to eat and I assign only what can be accomplished in twenty minutes to a half hour. Then the bulk of the housework is finished before the day is begun." In order to achieve this goal, you must be prepared to assign and oversee first thing in the morning.

Part of the chores assigned in a home with varied ages might be those of caring for younger siblings. You might pair an older child with a younger on a long-term basis, being careful to account for personalities that will mix well.

With young children, chores can be personal care tasks, such as brushing teeth, getting dressed, and straightening the bed — all before breakfast. If you can train your two-year-old to put on Velcro-closed shoes and zip his own jacket, that is two fewer things you will have to do in order to get out the door for a nature walk.

My mother-in-law has always hesitated to offer advice, but one of the pearls of parenting wisdom she has shared is that children need routines. It helps them to feel secure. Routine is absolutely essential for the management of a well-organized, efficient, and comfortable home. If you can establish a thoughtful management routine, you will greatly reduce your stress and your children's. Anticipate what will need to be done and think your tasks through in a logical manner. Spend more time teaching your children how to do household tasks than doing them for them. That will be time well-invested both in terms of work finished and, more importantly, personal relationships.

Atmosphere on the Bad Days

What about the bad days — the days when the environment is anything but picture perfect? Despite our best intentions and all our well-considered systems, life throws a curve ball occasionally and the system goes awry. Those are the days when it is most important to remember that our children are educated by their intimacies. A whole family together on a bad day is quite a laboratory for learning.

One such day occurred late in my last pregnancy. My husband was on a three-day business trip, and I was bound and determined that my house would be perfectly clean before the baby arrived. It was pouring rain — the perfect day for nesting. I got up early and decided to catch up on all laundry and to get the carpets clean. I put the load that I had washed at one o'clock a.m. (I couldn't sleep because I was afraid if I relaxed I'd go into labor without my husband) in the dryer and another in the washer. Then I made breakfast. I made dough for bread and set it to rise, feeling accomplished. While the children were eating, I went back down to the basement and transferred clothes from dryer to basket and washer to dryer.

I asked my ten-year-old, Michael, to carry up the carpet cleaner and carefully explained exactly what I wanted cleaned. Then I went back downstairs to the learning room/toy room/office to try to make order out of chaos. A short while later, Michael appeared, saying he was finished. I got him started folding laundry. Back upstairs, my three little children were watching Donut Man videos. I put the bread in the oven and discovered that the carpet was not clean at all. So I did it myself (not an easy task when one is nine months pregnant). I left the very heavy carpet cleaner with dirty water in it until Michael could help me empty it.

It was time to take the bread out of the oven. For some mysterious reason, all four loaves had risen to incredible heights and had a very strange texture. I fed everybody bread and peanut butter for lunch anyway. Now there were crumbs all over the clean carpet. I vacuumed. Thoroughly tired, I decided to try to take a nap. This was not a good idea because I could hear my sweet children arguing and disassembling the house.

Feeling defeated, I went back to the basement to fold more laundry and left the three little ones with the umpteenth playing of the Donut Man. A little voice (who sounded curiously like Charlotte Mason) kept whispering that videos are twaddle. I silenced the voice by telling her she'd never been nine months pregnant. In the silence, I heard a mysterious crash and hastily gathered a gigantic red bag of unmatched socks, thinking I'd better not leave my children unattended for the rest of the day. As I came upstairs with the socks, I heard Christian, who is six, muttering, "What am I going to tell her? Now I'm gonna be in big trouble...." Roughhousing, he had tripped over the carpet cleaner and dumped all the dirty water all over the clean carpet. I dropped the sock bag and spent the next half hour re-cleaning. Once it was all cleaned up I managed to speak sweetly to cowering Christian.

The rain had stopped. I asked Michael to empty the carpet cleaner and put it in the garage, and then to clean all the mud and dust from the previous day's soccer game out of the car. Michael went outside and the dog slipped out behind him. He chased the dog across the street, only to be confronted by a very unfriendly neighbor who yelled at him for not controlling his dog and threatened to call the authorities. Michael returned home in tears.

After calming him down and dispatching him to vacuum the car, I went back to the sock bag. Picking it up from where I had dropped it on the clean, wet carpet, I discovered that it was not colorfast! Now I had a gigantic red stain to clean. In the interim, Michael sneaked back up to his room with a book. After returning the carpet cleaner to the garage, I checked to make sure the carpet in the car was clean. It wasn't, so I did that myself.

Returning to the house, I caught Mary Beth, two, going potty on the kitchen floor. I cleaned that entire floor until it shone. Wearily, I decided to go downstairs and write my husband a long letter, telling him what he had missed (sometimes he gets sentimental about these trips and fears he's missing all the good times). About three minutes into my letter, Patrick, four, came down bawling. "Christian called me a dummy because I filled all the ice-cube trays to help you but I spilled them all over the floor." Giving up, I laughed hysterically at the absurdity of the entire day, thinking to myself that if the house had to be perfect before I went into labor we were never going to meet this baby.

No schooling happened that day, but much learning did. If our children are educated by their intimacies, there is nothing quite so intimate as being cooped up with a grouchy, pregnant mother on a rainy winter day. Our children are educated by each and every interaction with us and with their siblings. Knowing this, the typical home-educating mother would probably stop somewhere not too far into this kind of a day and remind herself to be sweet and charitable. That reminder will usually get her…nowhere. Home education is as much a parent's education as a child's. The mother needs to learn to be entirely dependent upon the Lord, and that lesson will take a lifetime. The bad days teach us humility. They teach us that without God we are noisy, clanging gongs, barking orders and losing tempers. Without Him, we cannot begin to accomplish the daunting task of educating our children in faith for life. With Him, we can do all things.

The bad days are the days that drive us to our knees. They are the days that form us. When Michele Quigley voiced her frustration over the bad days to her son Timothy, fourteen, he reminded her that He is the potter and we are the clay. Timothy went on to share that when we are young, we are soft and easily molded, but as we grow, we become more brittle. We mothers need to be chiseled instead of molded. That's why the bad days hurt so much. We can take those days, with all their imperfections, and place them at the foot of the cross. We can come before the crucified Lord, who suffered the ultimate bad day, and beg Him to chisel away our imperfections, to make us softer and mold us in His image. We can ask Him to educate us in an atmosphere of love.

Words from the Wise

Does the atmosphere in your home foster learning?

MacBeth Derham, New York

I think so. I hope so. It seems to, despite the near constant mess. I struggle with disorder, and that is my main source of frustration. Within the disorder, I do have some learning centers that must be kept neat…the bookshelves, the music shelves, and my bedroom are all neat. The bookshelves provide the children with easy access to materials; the music shelves provide the children with quick access to their instruments and sheet music. My bedroom provides them (and Mom) with a place to retreat when the rest of the house is overly cluttered.

Laurie Napolin, Delaware

I hope so. I like to have a quiet atmosphere but rarely do as I have two older daughters coming in and out a lot. I try to steer in a subtle way my daughter to doing constructive things such as sewing and crafts and reading but give her lots of time to just play. When my daughter has exciting things to show me in nature I always stop and look and grab the nature book to look it up. We listen to a lot of music since we don't play and have lots of craft stuff around and art books. We have a schoolroom upstairs because there is always something going on in the house with the older girls so it is easier to do school in a room but when things are quiet we curl up on the couch and read or else we read in the bedroom. I find my problem is I clean too much and yet feel I never get enough done so I have to let go and spend more time enjoying life.

What makes a day a "good day"?

MacBeth Derham, New York

A good day is a day when we all learn something new. Perhaps we start a new book, or perhaps we find something in our yard that wasn't there last week. Perhaps a child comes to me with a thought that makes me think. For instance, Elizabeth, my musical-mathematical child, came to me a few days ago after pondering two-dimensional space (really), and said, "You know, Mama, if we lived in two-dimensional space, we couldn't talk because sound waves are three dimensional." Trip, my visual-engineering child, has been writing and illustrating a series of spy books with his siblings and cousin as characters. He read some of them aloud at a recent talent show. He got so many compliments, that he wants me to look into publishing them. And the other children, too, bring me ideas... Annika laughs at the sandpipers and says they are just like her, running away from the waves after catching baby mole crabs, "...only I don't eat them!" she says. Ideas make a good day.

What is your management system in your home? Can it be refined to include your children more and to encourage them to grow in orderliness?

Willa Ryan, California

I have always been fairly casual and informal about requiring order. I don't like messes, but I also hate to tell a child he must take down the LEGO block construction he has spent the whole day building. It's always a balance, and I am afraid I am not so consistent as I should be. The main thing I am concentrating on now is excellence.

The children are in the habit of making their beds, picking up their rooms, bringing their dishes to the kitchen, etc., but now I am being a little stricter than before in expecting the jobs to be well done, not just done. I am trying to emphasize this more in their academic work too, more for their sake than mine — they are old enough now to be aware that they are doing less than their best. They protested at first, but now actually seem happier than when the standards were lower.

Trisha Artigues, Mississippi

I do laundry every Monday, Wednesday, and Friday. I do absolutely no laundry the other days of the week. I very early on decided that I hated doing some laundry every day and never having a break from it. It felt like something that never ended and I never had a feeling of accomplishment when I was doing it daily. On these days every bit of laundry is cleaned, folded, and put away. I have to add that I do have help and this makes the follow-through for everything much better. For cooking, I usually get away with cooking three big meals a week and eating leftovers the rest of the week and perhaps eating out once, but not always.

Barbara Rice, Virginia

We have chores listed on a dry erase board, and the children check off tasks as they are completed. I've always been a list maker, and they also seem to enjoy (be somewhat motivated by?) checking things off. They do not have many chores, but they are REAL — personal care (make bed) or things that really are a help (empty the dishwasher, clear the table, vacuum, etc.), not make-work. In fact, we started the two oldest on vacuuming (once a week — they pick the day) with a lightweight super broom, and that makes the house cleaner than it was, because I very rarely got around to it myself. I'm still training them in that, so I usually help clear the floors (especially the bedrooms), which encourages a weekly pickup.

I'm a food person, and have been through many good systems to make that area of home life run more smoothly. I've frozen multiple entrees ahead. I created a six-week cycle menu (no more, "What shall I make for dinner tonight?" at four o'clock p.m.). Right now, I'm in a dinner co-op with two other families. Every three months or so the moms get together and plan the menus and schedule. Tuesdays Anne brings dinner to Patty and me. Thursdays Patty brings dinner to Anne and me. Fridays or Saturdays I bring dinner to Anne and Patty. Between co-op meals and leftovers, I only need to cook a few days a week. (If you're considering starting one, try it for four weeks and keep in mind that it's easier with families of similar overall appetites and sizes, who live close to each other!)

MacBeth Derham, New York

I had a delightful stress-free week camping and beaching...and I made some discoveries about housekeeping and habit! Despite there being eight people staying in our camper that sleeps six, it was much easier to stay organized there than in our rather larger house. My captive audience was unable to escape the toothbrush monitor (me), as they often try to do. Since they were personally delivered to the bathroom, they all had to use the facilities before bed, so there were no midnight excursions to the bathroom (and no three-year-old accidents). Meals were planned, so if they refused to eat, there were no "alternative" meals. Television, which is never much of an issue anyway, was never even mentioned...except as we watched a camper full of small children across from us with a television — the mom tried to turn it off, and the children had horrible screaming fits.

How does clutter and materialism affect your home?

Michele Quigley, Pennsylvania

I think it can be difficult to figure out what is essential and what isn't. It's true you can look at just about everything and find a purpose for it...but purpose doesn't always equal necessity. In truth I think having a lot of "things" is a trick of Satan. Besides the whole materialistic aspect of it, there's the whole business of managing it all. I remember reading once that if Satan can't get you in sin, he'll get you in busyness. Managing a lot of "stuff" can keep you very busy (and very frustrated).

Willa Ryan, California

I'm trying to pray about it now that I recognize it as a moral issue. All I can think of is that the excess stuff in our house is a symptom of some bad habits of my family's. I am going to have to change some of my habits and ways of thinking before I can hope to make a real difference in the state of the house. I am going to be meditating on detachment and poverty of spirit. Perhaps the way to start would be to itemize what is really necessary as opposed to desirable. I know that when I am actually faced with something that is good and useful, but just not necessary, I have a hard time discarding it. Perhaps making a list of different categories — for example, clothing, bedding, curriculum, toys — and then figuring out what is the minimum we could get by with — would be a more positive way of approaching it.

Susanne Zinklar, Michigan

I am reminded of a vacation we were on when we stayed at our first condo/villa on the Gulf of Mexico. Life seemed so easy and wonderful even though I was cooking almost all of the meals, doing laundry, and keeping the villa tidy. We had tons of time for beach walks, swimming, reading, sleep. Could it have been because we had only that week's food in the fridge and cupboards, three outfits for each of us, a few games/toys/books to enjoy and only the toiletries absolutely needed?

How do you train the wills of your children? Do you use the same techniques with every child? Are they equally effective?

Barbara Rice, Virginia

My children are basically well behaved and receive compliments, but sometimes I despair of reaching their hearts and turning them to God. I think it's a lack in my own spiritual life. We use time-outs, loss of computer/video time, natural consequences and writing assignments (either the "I will not...." type or a salient Bible verse), but again this doesn't seem to reach the heart enough. Most of these are accompanied by a lecture/discussion. Sometimes we'll role play how to act/react or we'll pray together (for patience, etc.). My husband once jokingly said one son would stop hitting the other to avoid the lecture rather than the punishment! ("Who made David? Does God love David? How does God feel when you hit David? Why?")

Willa Ryan, California

I use the same general principles for every child, that is: obey your parents, be kind to each other, work before play, etc. But I do adjust my techniques a little to fit the child. I have one child who, though he is usually very respectful, occasionally has explosions of emotions where he acts inappropriately. I have found that sternness and punishment only raise his emotions to a higher pitch, while gentle, steady influence and kindness will soothe him and result in genuine penitence when his emotions fade. With another child, temper tantrums require a stern, no-nonsense manner. Of course, there are times when nothing seems to work. My mom's parenting advice comes in handy here, "Pray without ceasing."

How do you encourage curiosity and inquisitiveness in your home? Are you still inquisitive?

MacBeth Derham, New York

You mean, there are homes where inquisitiveness and curiosity are not encouraged? And some moms are not inquisitive? Goodness, everyone here is nosy — er — inquisitive! I think that is one of the things that makes cleaning and orderliness harder. Everything is interesting! The dust on the floor, the broken paintbrush, the twelve pieces of LEGO-that-can-be-made-

into-thirty-four-things that were under the bed, the feathers that sometimes come out of the pillow (goose?), the way the curtain frays (stop pulling!), the nice effect crayon has on patterned wallpaper, are all interesting things. I guess the idea is to train the curiosity to more productive ends.

Yet how do we raise young Edison without breaking his spirit? We do this by training his will, and turning it to a desire to do the right thing. We are still working on this.

Chari Bryan, California

The children here have lots of freedom to explore their world. We look things up when they have an interest or question. We look for unique ways to do or see things and they see me excited about lots of things. They are the only people I talk to most the time, so I have got to share my own discoveries with someone!

Barbara Rice, Virginia

We encourage inquisitiveness by being willing to drop things in pursuit of "butterflies." Like running outside with the field guide when a turtle is discovered, making a temporary cage/habitat, etc. My husband is home several mornings a week and will often instigate/participate in spur-of-the-moment projects. He and my dad spent an afternoon cutting a short path through the trees to make it easier to get to the creek, and I am amazed at how much time/fun/ exploring is going on now. I am finding more areas to explore for myself now that I've given up nearly all TV (more of a struggle for me than for some, I think).

After reading about discipline, what new habits will you endeavor to form in yourself this year? In your children?

Barbara Rice, Virginia

For myself I want to keep improving on my orderliness, organization, and follow-through. My desk pile was recently reduced, and I want to keep it that way. For the children (and this has been on my mind for MONTHS), I want to work on the habit of attention. This was a big problem with our more traditional curriculum last year and I wonder what will happen as we implement more Charlotte Mason methods this year.

MacBeth Derham, New York

This is one of my failings…I follow through until I see things getting done once, but forget that this is a long process. I need to inspect more. I need to show the children how to see the work through adult eyes, and teach them how to want things to look great. One of the things I like about Charlotte Mason is the focus on the parent — I need to work on my own habits, my own will, my own atmosphere, and then it will be easier to help the children. The children will not learn the fullness of the faith from an atheist, no matter how learned he is; no matter how he follows the rituals of the Church. Similarly, I cannot expect my little ones to learn the best habits without learning them myself.

If you had one piece of advice to someone starting out, what would it be?

Linda McDonough, Virginia

I asked an experienced mom this question four years ago when I started homeschooling. She answered, "Start your day with your house in order. If your house is out of order to begin with, your whole day will seem chaotic." I am not neat by inclination and our house can get out of control quickly! But if I start with things downstairs cleaned up the night before and then we make our beds and clean the upstairs before breakfast and school, everything runs so much more smoothly. The best book on the subject for creative types who tend toward disorder is **The Messies Manual** *by Sandra Felton. This book really changed my life!*

I have now moved on to the Don Aslett books and have read a number of others in between. I have spent the last three weeks de-cluttering in an attempt to get ready for the school year before going on vacation. I'm getting rid of all the twaddle and clutter and trying to simplify (which in many ways is what a Charlotte Mason education is all about). Let me tell you, it feels great! I just love watching all the junk pile up on curb and the feeling of walking into the basement and not tripping over anything. (Don Aslett says the best time to de-clutter is when you are packing for a long trip because you tend to take what you need — then it is easier to evaluate what's left over and get rid of what you don't need).

Battling Back from Burnout

Burnout occurs when we are out of sync with God. It happens when we shoulder a yoke that is not His. Some readers holding this book have been homeschooling for several years, following a prescribed educational plan that is not the right fit for their families. Some readers are just beginning to educate their children at home. While the advice in this chapter is directed to women in the throes of burnout, it has preventative value for women who are not burnt out.

A few years ago, I had a two-year experience which taught me a great deal about burnout. I want to share the lessons learned in this chapter. At the beginning of my journey, we sold and bought a house in what our realtor told us was the most chaotic, brutal real-estate transaction he'd ever witnessed. We moved into our new house and my husband started a new job that required him to work sixty-hour weeks and travel every weekend. Five months pregnant, and determined to be perfectly settled by the time the baby came, I unpacked by myself.

In August, I jumped into a very child-friendly hands-on curriculum with both feet. I started a unit study co-op with five other families and volunteered to teach the first five weeks.

In October, I had a baby.

In January, our dog died.

In February, I had a brutal case of pneumonia that lasted forever.

In May, we adopted a puppy. This puppy amazed my vet with the variety and intensity of intestinal parasites he tormented us with before he was housebroken.

In July, my husband, now totally exhausted from working sixty-hour weeks and traveling every weekend, spent several days in the hospital with a mysterious illness that resulted in the loss of his appendix.

Late in August, three days before school was to begin, I called every Catholic school within reasonable driving distance to see if anyone had kindergarten and third grade openings.

By the end of the day, I recognized that I had no good options. For the first time since our firstborn was an infant, I didn't feel like I was choosing to home educate — I felt like I was being forced to because I had no alternative. But I also felt certain that home education was the will of God for our family. And God knew that I was burnt out. So I took a leap of faith and begged God to help me turn things around. And I trusted that he would.

What is burnout? In her best-seller, *Simple Abundance*, Sarah Ban Breathnach writes:

> *It's burnout when you go to bed exhausted every night and wake up tired every morning — when no amount of sleep refreshes you, month after weary month. It's burnout when everything becomes too much effort: combing your hair, going out to dinner, visiting friends for the weekend, even going on vacation. It's burnout when you find yourself cranky all the time, bursting into tears or going into fits of rage at the slightest provocation. It's burnout when you dread the next phone call. It's burnout when you feel trapped and hopeless, unable to dream, experience pleasure, or find contentment. It's burnout when neither the big thrills nor the little moments have the power to move you — when nothing satisfies you because you haven't a clue what's wrong or how to fix it. Because everything's wrong. Because something's terribly out of whack: you.*

I know that my experience with burnout is not an isolated one for Catholic home educators. We are women who give until it hurts. Catholic homeschooling mothers are women who embrace sacrifice and offer it up. Frequently, moms who are educating their children at home are women who spend an entire decade or more either pregnant or postpartum. They are women who have not slept through the night — any night — in ten years. They are women who, when the neighbor ladies leave the bus stop in the morning to share a cup of tea together, hunker down in their own dining rooms with their own small band of children to begin the school day. Home educators are women who spend all day, every day meeting the needs of small, medium, and large children — sometimes all at once. In the home-education community beat the hearts of women of extraordinary faith who are laying down their lives for their families.

While that sacrifice to fulfill Christ's mission for this life is wholly appropriate, sacrificing at the altar of perfectionism, overcommitment, and disorganization most decidedly is not.

You must take care of yourselves as well as you take care of your families. The home education community needs your hearts to keep beating. Your children need you healthy, whole, and sane. Your mission needs you. And your mission is so very important because your children are the future of the Church and the brightest hope for a troubled world.

Even if you are burnt out, there is a faint flicker of hope stirring in your soul. You want to recover. Where do you begin? As with every undertaking, small or large, you begin with prayer. Set aside fifteen minutes at the beginning of each day to be alone to meditate. Do whatever it takes. Barricade your door. Pray in the shower. Go for a walk. Just be sure that you do it every day and that you are alone with your Lord. Put yourself in the presence of the Holy Spirit and ask him to help you heal your charred and weary soul and body.

Pray for inspiration and listen to His whisperings with complete confidence that there lies the power to battle back from burnout. Remember that the power that you are seeking is the same power that created the universe out of nothing; it is the same power that parted the Red Sea. It is the power that conceived a savior in the womb of a virgin. It is the power that raised the Messiah from the dead.

Engrave Philippians 4:13 upon your heart; it is your motto for battling back: "I can do all things through Christ who strengthens me."

Your next step is to begin to create order out of the inevitable chaos of burnout. If you do not have one, buy a planner. Go tomorrow — regardless of what month it is — planning is key. I like the Seven Habits planner put out by Franklin Covey.

Right now, the first rule of use for your planner is accept no new commitments. Learn to say "No, I'm sorry. I have a prior obligation." Because you do. You have an obligation to yourself and your recovery. Used properly, the Covey planner forces you to sit down weekly and commit to paper at least one thing that you will do in each of four areas — physical, mental, emotional, and spiritual — to nurture yourself. Covey likens this to sharpening the saw. You can cut wood with a dull saw, but it is an arduous task. How much better would it be to take the time to sharpen the saw?

Using the Covey planner, you will be forced to chart a compass for your journey to full recovery from burnout. Once you have sharpened the saw, you are to define the roles you play and to set goals for each of them. Finally you are to commit to paper each week how you meet those goals. You absolutely must organize your time. This plan will become your prescription for healing. This is a gold mine, my friends, permission to take care of yourself.

If you are recovering from burnout, I am going to take the pressure off by suggesting appropriate goals in each area to aid your restoration.

First to sharpen the saw.

Chances are, for the first few weeks, your physical goal should be to get more sleep. Find a way to take a nap every day and then make sure you do it. Be creative; there is a way. And it is of utmost importance. In her classic *The Reed of God*, Caryl Houselander writes: "One of our commonest natural experiences of the sense of loss is tiredness: it empties us out; it is almost as if we had let the infant fall from our tired hands. It is useless to flog a tired mind, useless to reproach a tired heart; the only way to God when we are tired out, is the simplest wordless act of faith."

In the fall, when I was trying to discern what had gone so wrong that I was left burnt out, a friend reminded me of the way I take care of myself when I'm pregnant. She said, "You eat perfectly — no sugar, nothing refined, no caffeine. You measure protein in grams to be sure you get enough every day. You take really good vitamins and you never miss a day. You nap daily without apology. You exercise daily and enjoy it. You ask for help. You do this because you know that to take care of yourself well is to take care of your baby well. Then the baby is born and you push your needs aside to meet the needs of the baby and all his newly displaced siblings. You would be better able to meet the needs of that baby and the rest of the family if you could recognize that to take of yourself postpartum and throughout their childhood is just as important as taking caring of yourself during pregnancy. It's like the old analogy of the plane crash. If the plane is going down, put your oxygen mask on before you help your child. You can't help him if you pass out."

You can't help your children if you're burnt out. I am giving you permission today to take care of your physical well-being every day from this day forward.

Perhaps your mental goal will be to get outside everyday. How is this a mental goal? The outdoors will clear your mind. God is so present in nature. Every day, *every* day, take the children and go outside. Walk in the rain, in the snow, in the early morning sunshine of a hot July day.

October 2002
We spent the day at the pumpkin farm. This is school Cool!

    Early in my battle back from burnout, someone suggested I "let Mother Nature nurture." Honestly, I dismissed this suggestion as a New-Age hippie slogan. However, it came to mind most readily when I was teaching religion to a group of small children a few weeks later. We were discussing Creation, and I was telling them the story in sequence, reading from Genesis and commenting as I read. When I got to the sixth day, I stopped and pointed out to the children how the world was created and waiting in all its splendor for God's greatest creation. We looked at pictures of mountains and oceans and animals and plants. They were impressed that God made all those beautiful things for them to enjoy.

    Over the next few days, I reflected upon how little time I spent outside. I spend lots of time caring for God's most beautiful creations but most of that time is spent indoors (or in the car). Suddenly, I had an urge to hike in the mountains, to visit a farm, and to plant flowers.

    When we moved, I thought we were moving to the country, and I envisioned a slower pace in a nearly rural setting. Instead, it seems that half the world moved with us and our little town isn't rural at all. We moved to "the country" but I spent much time driving east, toward the city. Not exactly an antidote to stress.

    I discovered that I can just as easily drive west and be immersed in God's country. The mountains are beautiful and the farms as picturesque as a postcard. It is so easy to see the hand of God in the beauty and majesty of the natural world. It is also much easier to pray when one escapes the busy motion of city life.

I have also noticed that my children are much more peaceful in the big outdoors. They love to climb trees, jump creeks, and go "mountain climbing" (hike on very tame trails in mountainous parks). We all come home rested in mind as well as in spirit.

Does Mother Nature nurture? Not exactly. But the gentle hand of God touches us all as surely as the afternoon sun and the gentle summer rain tenderly kiss our faces.

Get outside; clear your head. In no time, you'll be thinking good thoughts. My time outside was my first taste of the Charlotte Mason–inspired lifestyle that I know God intended for me.

Your emotional goal absolutely should be to find time to be alone.

In her book, *The Charlotte Mason Companion*, Karen Andreola writes:

> *Before she marries, a young lady does not imagine herself facing the difficulties of managing the complicated workings of a household. Untried responsibilities come upon her as soon as she does marry. And, perhaps, just as she is grasping the situation, her first child is born and fills her whole heart. Then, not only her own health but that of another's depends on how she manages her life. The question of child training and how to bring up children becomes a new study and practical concern.*
>
> *Another child is born who eventually becomes a sunny companion for the first. But it seems that with each passing year, a mother's job description is revised. The desire for her husband's love and friendship is still strong, but a careful division of her attention is given up to the various aspects of maintaining a happy, well-managed home. Time alone with her husband now seems to have to be either previously planned moments or stolen ones. There are holiday celebrations to arrange, extended family parties and visits, church functions, occasions for neighborly hospitality, etc. In the center of it all is one little woman — wife, mother, mistress all in one: As the children approach their years of more formal education, there is the organization of the home schoolroom, and thus she walks over new ground again.*

Karen continues,

> *Is it a wonder she feels overspent? She wears herself out. In her efforts to be dietitian, laundress, nurse, hostess, teacher, taxi driver, wife, mother, and mistress, she forgets that she needs a little time for herself. And it is then that she stops growing spiritually and mentally. Physically, she feels ragged and drags through the day until, without being able to mark the hour it began, she lives with depression. Her mind is in a drifting fog when she wants it to think clearly and efficiently. With the distractions of her multi-faceted duties she is unable to follow a train of thought. She considers herself hopelessly behind in everything. Her feet are in quagmire. It takes an incredible effort to keep up appearances, to wear a winsome countenance. The last straw is the guilt she feels that she is lukewarm in the Lord.*

Karen goes on to suggest spending time alone reviving yourself. Among her personal favorite ways to spend time are: field trips for Mom, time spent in a museum, enjoying good art or time at a concert, immersed in good music; time spent gardening; time engaged in stimulating conversation with other adults; time spent in prayer. Another suggestion is to keep three books going, in addition the Bible: a stiff book, a moderately easy book, and a novel — always take up whichever you feel fit for. She calls this time "Mother Culture" and Charlotte Mason referred to "Teacher Culture." These times are necessary for the teacher to bring a freshness and perspective to education.

I am not suggesting large chunks of time away, particularly if you have children under three — just a few stolen hours here and there with Dad or Grandma or a willing godparent to hold down the fort. This is the most difficult of all goals for me to fulfill. I am very attached to my family and have trouble separating. Yet I know that our Lord has provided the example of time alone and I know that ultimately it benefits my family.

Consider the spiritual goal Edith Stein sets forth for women: "The soul of a woman must therefore be expansive and open to all human beings; it must be quiet so that no small weak flame will be extinguished by stormy winds; warm so as not to benumb fragile buds; clear, so that no vermin will settle in dark corners and recesses; self contained, so that no invasions from without can impede the inner life; empty of itself, in order that extraneous life may have room in it; finally, mistress of itself and also of its body, so that the entire person is readily at the disposal of every call" (*Woman*, 132-133). She does not describe a burnt-out woman; she describes a fully recollected one.

To work toward this end, your spiritual goal for the entire recovery period will remain the same. Bookend the day with prayer. Begin with the meditation time I already spoke of and end with a time to reflect. What went right that day? What went wrong? Make an earnest act of contrition and ask for grace to right the wrongs. Open your planner at day's end and glance over what you accomplished. Transfer the incompleted items to the following day if appropriate. Then, on the page of the day that is ending, write down five things for which you are grateful. This is not a lengthy journal entry, just a short five-item list. Here are two days' examples from my own journal, each reflecting a different attitude:

March 29
1. Aveeno baths
2. Aveeno lotion
3. Herbal tea
4. Donut Man videos at two a.m. with Mary Beth when nothing else will distract from the itching
5. Naps

April 18
1. Bible study with the neighbors
2. Good children during Bible study
3. Christian's smile and Paddy's eyes
4. Freshly laundered sheets
5. Time alone with Mike after everyone is asleep

This discipline fosters gratitude. Over time, when you know that you are to be accountable to your gratitude journal, you begin to look for things to record. Slowly, you nurture a grateful heart.

When gratitude meets prayer at the end of the day, truly remarkable things begin to happen. To bring a list of things for which we are grateful before the throne of the One who created the universe is to truly give thanks. When we develop a habit of thanking the Lord for the blessings He generously bestows, we become ever more aware of those blessings and of God's magnitude and his generosity. It really is a beautiful, grace-filled world. Those are your four personal goals:

- To rest more and to take excellent care of your physical body.
- To spend some time outdoors daily.
- To make time to be alone.
- And to begin your day invoking the power of the Holy Spirit and end it with heartfelt gratitude.

Now let's look at the roles you play and how they have fueled the fire of your burnout. Covey's planning sheet provides space for seven roles. For a mother educating her own children, those goals are pretty well defined. Since you are burnt out and it hurts to think, I am going to suggest some appropriate goals for each role for the next few weeks.

Your first role is that of a Christian, walking in a personal relationship with Christ. This role is separate from that of an apostle. I have found that our roles are interlaced — we don't stop wearing one hat when we don another — but it does help to artificially separate them for the purpose of clearing our vision. In order to nurture your relationship with our Lord, you must spend time with Him. Read Scripture and meditate upon it daily. Do it early in the day so that you can reflect upon it as you go about your daily round.

Seek the Lord in the sacraments frequently. I suggest this with some trepidation. The idea is not to fill your calendar with more to-dos when you are feeling exhausted and overwhelmed. The winter I had pneumonia, I bundled up four children daily and hustled off to nine o'clock Mass. Once there I had to hold my twenty-two-pound four-month-old the entire time while my chest burned and my head pounded. By the time I got home I was too tired to begin school and it was only ten o'clock. Practice prudence. Ask the Lord for solutions. You need the sacraments, but if you are truly burnt out you do not need extra physical and tactical burdens. In hindsight, I think I should have settled for one daily Mass during the week when I could duck out and leave my little ones with a neighbor. With time, as you regain your footing, you can add more devotions to your schedule, and you will discover that they refresh you rather than burden you.

I also strongly recommend that you seek spiritual direction. The crushing fatigue of burnout makes one vulnerable to spiritual nonsense. A competent spiritual director can show you how God plans to create good from a situation that appears very bad indeed. Trust that, if you seek Him, God will shed light on your current darkness, and He will make your recovery from burnout a time of tremendous personal growth.

Your next role is one of a wife. Share the definition of burnout with your husband. Talk to him about your needs for recovery. This is something I highly recommend. I think it is an absolute requirement if you are to recover. In his book *Men Are from Mars, Women Are from Venus*, John Gray writes that women need to be protected; they want someone to come alongside and take care of them. Conversely, men need to protect. They want to be protectors. So why isn't this the perfect match?

Because a woman waits until she is exhausted and frustrated before she blurts out every need that isn't being met in an angry tirade or flood of uncontrollable sobbing. This outburst of helplessness and hopelessness frightens and overwhelms a man so that he cannot meet her needs. How much better it would be to plan to sit down and discuss in a rational manner where we need help — practically, spiritually, and emotionally.

Marriage is the complete joining of two lives. If one of you is burnt out, you both suffer terribly. Women may be surprised to discover that their spouses are also burnt out. You truly are one body. My husband and I discovered that we both had crashed and burned and that we were handling it differently.

The night I shared the definition of burnout with my husband, he looked at me with eyes that said, "You understand. Finally someone knows how I feel." Truthfully, this was about two months after I had discovered the definition and was working in my own life to recover. His case seemed more serious at the time and it wasn't until much later — after he quit that job and had had time to recover — that I asked him to help me.

Women who educate their children at home seem to have very independent natures. We don't easily ask for help. We don't easily articulate our needs to the men in our lives. We must cultivate that skill. It is important to our health and the health of our marriages. This is a journey we travel together. We need to help each other navigate. You are not weak or inadequate if you need your husband's help to care for your family or educate your children. You are married.

The best weeks in our household are the ones in which my husband and I sit down together and look at our roles and goals and our plans to meet those goals. We help each discern what is important and what is not and how we can work together to achieve the ends we desire.

Your next role is that of a mother. This is separate from your role as a teacher. My goal for you in this realm is a very simple one. Be a friend to your children. Treat your children, no matter how young, as if they were your best friends. To some of you, this advice will seem too liberal and a sure prescription for poor parenting. Please let me explain.

When your first baby was born, chances are you treated him with the utmost kindness and careful respect. I'm willing to bet that child never heard you yell for the first couple of years. But as he grew and you added to your family, as the pressure to meet the needs of many individuals mounted, you became a taskmaster. The focus in your relationship shifted in subtle waves over time. Now, you are utterly exhausted and those relationships you hold most dear have deteriorated.

We are in authority over our children. God put us there. That does not mean that we must be tyrants. That does not give us license to berate, belittle, or scream at them. That does not allow us to excuse our own weakness and impatience. Remember: Charity, above all. Be a friend to your child. Listen with interest. Speak with courtesy. Think of him as a friend. When he behaves in a way that would not be desired in your best friend, speak the truth in love. Must you correct or admonish? Of course you must. For this is a child. And while he is your friend, he is still growing. You must shape him so that he is a good friend.

Shortly before he died, Col. Mike Pennefather, who was known in our local Catholic community as an exemplary father and a wonderful friend to the homeschooling community, wrote an article in which he referred to his seven grown children as his "best friends on this planet." What an incredible tribute! With that simple phrase — best friends on this planet — he speaks both of the beauty of their relationship and of the integrity and worth of his children.

Think of working toward that goal. Yes, we need to form our children. We want them to be worthy and loving friends. We absolutely need to guide them with loving firmness. And we need to nurture and cultivate our relationship with them. We need to be good friends to them so that they learn how to be good friends. I am not advocating that you relinquish authority. To do so would be to plunge your children into a sea of confusion and bewilderment. I am simply advocating that you treat children with the respect and gentleness of an excellent mentor, an older and wiser friend, whose strength is that she inspires the heart of her student.

Plums
Oct. 2002
M. Renita See

What does this have to do with burnout? Everything. When you treat your children as treasured friends, so much of the tension that has built in your household will dissipate. You will begin to relax and enjoy your role as a mother. You will recapture the exuberance and innocence of those early days. You will once again delight in the humorous antics and refreshing sweetness of little children. You will savor long and interesting conversations with a young teenager who is just beginning to make sense of the world. Mama will be happier, and so will her children. You will find that you are more patient; you explain your requests more completely and the compliance necessary for the smooth running of your household will follow naturally.

Now let's examine your other role with your children — that of teacher. Find support. You don't need a giant group as much as you need one other mother who can lift you up. Be careful that this person does not allow you to wallow in self-pity. The best support person will offer empathy, encouragement, humor, and a spiritual kick in the pants. Maybe not all at once but certainly over time. Practically speaking, you need to have someone with whom you can leave your children during school hours when you occasionally need time to yourself — for a doctor's appointment, to spend time alone in church, or to spend several hours dejunking your house.

E-mail support is wonderful. You can read and contribute according to your time and energy, and there is a vast diversity of ideas to be tapped. Share freely. Glean wisdom wholeheartedly. You need someone to share homeschooling ideas and resources with. But be careful. No matter how much you love and respect your homeschooling buddies, you must keep your eyes on your own work. Design your educational environment to reflect your philosophy and the needs and aptitudes of your children. To do anything less is to shortchange yourself of one of the greatest joys and blessings of home education. The curriculum must serve you and your children, not the other way around. This takes soul-searching. You need to really take a good long look at your learning style, your children's learning styles, your teaching style, and perhaps most importantly, your lifestyle. For years, the former classroom teacher in me kept trying to re-create the perfect kindergarten in my own home.

Because of the nature of my husband's work, we have one of the most unpredictable schedules I know. I'm not a high-energy person, and I have a low tolerance for extreme messiness. Heavy-preparation, high-activity, super-messy curricula fed my burnout. On the other hand, a highly structured packaged curriculum would inspire perfectionism and feed my burnout. It has taken years, but I have found a comfortable learning and teaching style that suits our family. Now, I approach the fall of a new home-education year with relaxed anticipation. It feels great.

So what's my style? It is a learning-lifestyle education, approached prayerfully, and tailored to my children. My style isn't what is important. What is your style? Don't buy another book, another manipulative, until you take a good, long, prayerful look at yourself, your family, your home, and your goals. What approach suits you? You have your pick. Choose wisely.

While you are considering curriculum, look at the rhythms of daily life in your house. Plan, as much as possible, a logical sequence of daily events. I am not talking about an airtight schedule. Airtight schedules where you feed the baby for thirty minutes at the top of the hour, then play for ten, then put him down for a nap and read to the toddler and the four-year-old for twenty minutes, then set them playing quietly for the next twenty minutes while you teach long division, are just going to set you up for failure. Don't be a slave to your schedule or your clock. Instead, work with the natural rhythm of life in your household to set up comfortable, logical, manageable routines. I am talking about taking the stress out of the things that are to be repeated every day like meals, dressing, lesson time, and chores by seeing where they fit together, and then helping your family to find its rhythm. The rhythms and routines of daily life provide comfort and security to the entire family. They remove the need for constant decision-making over things that should be habits and are the oil that lubricates a well-run homeschooling household.

Now, on to your role as homemaker. If you are a veteran home educator, you have heard the clutter talks. You have heard the meals-in-the-freezer talks. You have heard how chores shape character and keep your house clean. You know that home educators have to be efficient homemakers. If you missed those talks, borrow them on tape from a veteran. They are full of wise advice. I once heard that there are only two kinds of large families: very well-organized ones or hopelessly chaotic ones. With many children, there is no middle ground. I think we can take that a step farther. In homeschooling households, large or small, where children are home all day, every day, there is no middle ground. We must be efficient homemakers. You have a responsibility to educate yourself regarding the management of a household. I highly recommend Denise Schoefield's books for this purpose. But don't read them this week or next. Give yourself some time to recover first. You don't need a huge project right now. Later, read and implement them as necessary.

But I want to address the burnt-out mom who has read all the books and listened to all the advice and tried to do it all efficiently and is exhausted. It always frustrates me to hear experienced mothers advise novices to train their children to clean the house. They outline the merits of chores and character training. Then they spend the next forty-five minutes extolling the virtues of eight-, ten-, and twelve-year-olds who are extremely capable, competent, and virtuous. It is all true. It is all wonderful. But it is no consolation to the mother of five children who are seven and under and needs help now — this year. If this is your situation, no matter how well you train them, you are going to have to bear the brunt of the burden yourself.

This reality really came home to me one summer a few years ago. During the summer, we invite a child from Belfast to live with us. This particular summer, we had a delightful child named Carl staying with us. He became a fast friend of my nine-year-old. He also was capable of cleaning the kitchen, running the vacuum efficiently, and doing any other chore that was previously reserved for nine-year-old Michael to do alone. Suddenly, I had two sets of children: the older and the younger. The older could put the kitchen in sparkling order while I bathed the younger and put them to bed. The older could be trusted to efficiently tidy and clean the basement while I napped with the younger. It didn't take them long. It wasn't an unfair burden dumped on one child. It was a relatively quick, simple task.

Then our Irish visitor went home. And it was business as usual for me — battling the fatigue and nausea of the first trimester of a new pregnancy — and my one older child. We returned to an unequal balance of competent helpers to mess-makers.

Here are some potential coping strategies for those of us who are still primarily responsible for housekeeping:

Hire help. The first time I heard this, I laughed. Who can afford to hire help? But as Ginny Seuffert writes in *Catholic Home Schooling*: "This is also the time to point out a fact that many hard-working Christian women are hesitant to admit: there is no disgrace in hiring domestic help. The year I began home schooling, I used the money we had been spending on tuition and had a cleaning lady come in two or three times each week." I could have kissed the page when I read that. I could not have a cleaning lady two or three times a week, but we did hire help twice a month for a few months last year just to get us past the roughest spots.

I have a friend who had her fifth baby just before her oldest turned seven. On the morning before Christmas, two cleaning ladies appeared at her front door and explained that they would return every other week. Merry Christmas! Love, her husband. There is a man who understands burnout. There is a man who is close to the heart of his wife. These are not people of great means, but he looked at the cost effectiveness of cleaning help and found it a reasonable investment.

When we had three little children and a smaller house, my husband would take the boys, pick up his father, and go to the grocery store once a week, detailed list in hand. Granddad, Daddy, and the boys usually stopped for donuts on the way home, visited with Grandma for a while, and had a grand time. What was I doing? Speed cleaning. I'd load the stereo with Amy Grant and blitz through that house, reveling in the time alone. I enjoyed putting things in order, making things shine. I found peace in my well-ordered home. Mike would return home, we'd have a full refrigerator and pantry, the boys were happy, the grandparents were happy, the house was clean, and I was feeling fine.

Take a look at your assets. That solution worked well for us because Mike is good at grocery shopping and actually enjoyed taking the boys to do what most consider a burdensome task. At that point in our lives, I would have rather cleaned the house by myself, my way, than sit down with him and divide chores.

If Dad is unavailable to take the children out, can you hire a young teenager to play in the yard for an hour a couple of times a week? Can you trade off with another homeschooling mom?

That the chores must be done is not negotiable.

You must clear out the clutter. You must streamline and simplify your homemaking. Not today. Not tomorrow. But someday in the near future. We need time to order our environments. We need to make time and space for beauty.

Amidst the unceasing demands of little ones, unwavering deadlines, and the stress of daily life there have been moments, many moments, when I have wished I were living in a monastery. Wouldn't it be simpler to be more prayerful, more contemplative, and more peaceful in the quiet and order of a hermitage instead of being in the midst of a large family? Strangely enough, as I leafed through a monastery cookbook looking for a recipe that could easily be quadrupled, I stumbled upon this quote from *The Long Rules of St. Basil:* "In the midst of our work we can fulfill the duty of prayer, giving thanks to him who has granted strength to our hands for performing our tasks and cleverness to our minds for acquiring knowledge, and for providing the materials."

This concept appeals to me enormously: to pray unceasingly through the work of my ordinary days, to consecrate the little things and so to live joyfully in the continual presence of God. I am not new to the idea of doing more than one thing at a time. Early in my mothering adventure, it was an idea suggested to me often. Experienced voices sang the praises of cleaning the bathroom while supervising a child's bath, making a phone call while emptying the dishwasher, and my favorite, listening to books on tape while doing the housework. I even have a postpartum exercise book that suggests the following:

"Start your pliés in the bathroom as you finish your bicep curls — then go to the bathroom. Go to the sink and do the wall push and the tricep extension while continuing to work your legs...Do the kinetic pushups standing up. Now do your calf raises while brushing your teeth. Then wash your face and continue with the pliés and some kegals. Next turn on the shower and while it's getting hot, do twenty-five to fifty controlled crunches. Take a shower."

One can see how the idea of dovetailing can easily get out of hand. One morning, as I was brushing my teeth and supervising a youngster in the tub, I tried to answer the phone and make the bed. It didn't work. After finishing at the sink, concluding the phone call, and toweling and dressing my son, it dawned on me that I might be taking efficiency a bit too far. In my effort to do as much as possible with a day that seemed too short, I was missing opportunities to sanctify the moment.

If we shatter time into tiny fragments we cannot be fully present in it. We cannot be conscious that our work is a prayer and find the sacred in the ordinary. We cannot feel the presence of God. To go even further, if we bustle along at this pace, we are not readily available to the people in our lives either. And, finally, we are on the short track to burnout, the inability to see, or hear, or feel, or sense the joy that is abundantly present in everyday life. We are simply too tired, too stressed, too preoccupied.

Returning to the ridiculous exercise quote, my most fruitful prayers are ones I pray while walking in the early morning. The rhythm of my feet and the wheels of the stroller in front of me, the quiet of the morning and the sounds of God's creation in nature all work in harmony to bring together a blending of body and spirit. But this requires full time and attention to the purpose of my walking meditation. It is entirely different from cramming in as many crunches as possible before the water gets hot.

One of the best ways to experience joy in a house full of children is to pretend you are a monk. Sanctify your movements. All of them. Slow them down. Be aware of your purpose. Give thanks for your chores. Make them holy. Make them happy.

Women need to learn that housework isn't drudgery, it's sacred. It's creative. We need time to create — whether it is a well-cooked meal, fragrant loaf of bread, bright, jewel-colored jars of homemade preserves neatly decorating our pantry, a warm hand-knit afghan, a lovely heirloom scrapbook, or a well-tended garden. We need to glorify the Creator and refresh our souls by creative endeavors of abundant homemaking. Get the dreary details under control so that you can live life in your home as abundantly as our Lord intended.

In her book of meditations, *Being Home*, Gunilla Norris writes: "Prayer and housekeeping — they go together. They have always gone together. We simply know that our daily round is how we live. When we clean and order our homes, we are somehow also cleaning and ordering ourselves. We know this by virtue of being human creatures. How we hold the simplest of our tasks speaks loudly about how we hold life itself."

Take this to heart. Go about your daily round with an attitude of service, an air of peace. Homemaking is very creative. It's hard to think of scrubbing sinks and washing diapers that way, but you can make holy even the most mundane of tasks when you approach them with a spirit of prayer and of love — love for your Creator, who loves you abundantly, and love for your family for whom you are working so hard.

Now, a word about the telephone — that tool which shatters domestic tranquility. My friend Heidi Spinelli has said that when she has a bad day she talks on the phone a lot — or is it the other way around? Look at the phone from the perspective of the people around you. They cannot see or hear the person to whom you are talking, they are not a part of the chatter and the laughter; they are definitely being ignored. Would you have an extended phone conversation with someone else if your neighbor were in your house? Would you chatter with an acquaintance while you held your beloved? Noooo....

But do you have extended conversations while your children are about, often misbehaving in an effort to get your attention? Do you chatter in the dark while you nurse your baby to sleep? In the end, isn't this more stressful than not? Wouldn't it be better just to relax and enjoy some quiet time with that sweet, warm baby? Here again, we sanctify the moment instead of shattering it. Learn to use the answering machine, the caller ID, and best of all, e-mail. Remember, treat your children with the respect and courtesy you would your friends. They will learn the same courtesy.

Finally, you are an apostle in the world. I put this role last because I believe that your roles as a Catholic wife, a mother, a teacher, and a homemaker comprise your primary apostolate. When you plan apostolic endeavors, remember your primary apostolate. Resist the urge to overcommit to every good and worthwhile endeavor, leaving your children in grave danger of becoming apostolic orphans. Be discerning in your choice of apostolates. Strive for balance.

Pay careful attention to apostolic works you can do from home. These are powerful witnesses to your children. To this end, I gather the neighborhood children twice a week for religious instruction. A great benefit to this is that there no longer exists an artificial separation of church friends and neighborhood friends for my children.

I also offer a Bible study for neighborhood women weekly in my living room. It is mentally challenging and spiritually enriching for me, and the women tell me that they have learned more about their faith in the last eighteen months than in the previous thirty years.

We are each called to different apostolic works depending on our gifts, our temperaments, our health, and the needs of our families. When we look carefully at these characteristics we can discern what it is that God wants us to do. He knows those characteristics. For us to ignore them and plow ahead because we consider a cause virtuous is to risk missing God's whisper.

God does not want you to be ill, exhausted, angry, and frustrated. If you are burnt out, He is providing an opportunity for you to examine your life and His call. In summary:

- Remember to sharpen the saw.
- Take care of yourself physically, as if you were caring for a precious child within — you are. That child is you, beloved daughter of God.
- Nurture your emotional health by spending time alone.
- Drink in the beauty of the natural world and thereby clear your mind.
- Begin your day asking for the help and grace of God, and end it with gratitude.
- In your role as a Christian, take time to build a personal relationship with Christ through prayer and the sacraments.
- Seek spiritual direction.
- In your role as a wife, share with your husband the definition of burnout and your struggles with it. Share honestly how you want him to help you.
- In your role as a mother, be a friend to your children.
- In your role as a teacher, seek a homeschooling friend with whom to share burdens and joys. Discern prayerfully what your true teaching and lifestyles are and then make the curriculum work for you. Be sure to take time for teacher workdays alone.
- In your role as a homemaker, determine what you can do alone reasonably and then come up with ways to get help with the rest.
- Find the rhythm you need to establish routines in all four roles: wife, mother, teacher, and homemaker.
- As an apostle, strive for healthy balance, and look for opportunities to serve from your home or with your children beside you. Do not make apostolic orphans of your children.

Stephen Covey likens living according to your personal compass, such as the one outlined above, to taking a plane trip. You will not be on course the whole time. You won't even be on course most of the time, but if you keep coming back to the plan; you will arrive at your destination. The ultimate destination is heaven. Remember that our Lord is your navigator. Consult Him continuously. I wish you Godspeed on your journey.

Words from the Wise

Do you think the learning lifestyle approach works well if Mom is pregnant or there is a new baby in the house? How does it work better than other approaches?

Willa Ryan, California

I've been homeschooling for almost five years, wondering when everything would finally settle down so I could actually do real homeschooling. Sometimes I get anxious about the future. But why would God call us to homeschool if He knew we couldn't do it? So I feel He must be using these crises and confusions to prepare my children and myself for something that He needs us to be prepared for. Who knows what it will be? Who except God really knows why He is calling so many to homeschool, often under difficult circumstances. I'm sure the Israelites out in the wilderness bringing up children had to walk in faith too, not knowing what life in the Promised Land would hold for their children; all they knew was that God had promised to be with them always.

In a way, Charlotte Mason methods of gathering together, reading good books, and getting outdoors to observe natural history has been our way of responding to pregnancy/new baby times when I often feel quite unsure what the next moment will bring. I wonder sometimes if God uses these times to gently remind me why I am really bringing my children up at home. After all, we are scripturally instructed to bring our children up "in the nurturing and admonition of the Lord" and this should be a natural (though not always simple) process, not an artificial one. Sometimes a new little one is just the thing to show a mother and siblings what nurture and admonition are all about!

My problem in the past has been that I thought of reading, and getting outdoors as habit-forming and as nice extras, but not really what homeschooling was all about. I'd get into this cycle: plan a schedule, start imposing the schedule on all of us, feel good about it and start piling on more formal work, then end up juggling too many plates and feeling discouraged when they eventually all came crashing down. Then I'd basically plumb the depths for a while, feeling very inadequate as a mother, and then start just relating to my children again by reading and spending time with them. Then eventually, when things were more stable, I'd feel it was time to get back to the real thing — and start writing out schedules again. The whole cycle would be repeated.

This time I'm trying to keep my vision a little clearer and avoid the extremes of overscheduling and crashing into burnout. We don't get to "school" every day, but we do usually manage to maintain the "pegs" and basic routine that keeps us thriving and involved in the family life.

I've tried structured schooling with my children while pregnant, and I've tried radical unschooling (what Charlotte Mason calls "laissez aller" or just letting go!) and now I'm trying the Charlotte Mason approach, which to me seems like a middle ground between the two.

And so far it seems to be working the best.

A Final Thought
Educated by Our Intimacies

The opportunity to educate our children at home is a precious blessing. When we spend large quantities of time listening to each other, working together, and enjoying one another we build a lovely family culture. It is within this culture, in the safe shelter of the domestic church, that we begin to change the world for Christ.

Charlotte Mason repeatedly reminds us that we are educated by our intimacies. This wise observation is no less true for adults than for children. Parents who invest themselves in their children are afforded a priceless opportunity to grow in grace. We are educated by the intimate relationships we have with the souls entrusted to us.

Children who live a lifestyle of learning are educated by the intimate relationships they have with their parents and with their siblings. These relationships are unique to families who have chosen to keep their children at home when other children go to school. Home-educating families make tremendous sacrifices; they reap tremendous benefits. Over time, the latter far outdistance the former. Seeking to understand one another, to see Christ in each other, and to enrich each other with living ideas will be our path to heaven.

The books we share, the art we enjoy, the music we listen to will all become part of the tapestry woven into the blanket which will envelop us even as we grow and undertake worthy pursuits apart from each other. What we do, the lifestyle we lead, is who we are — as a family and as individuals. Our relationships with what we study will shape us. Our relationships with whom we love will bring God's glory to that shape. It may have been academics which first led us to home education; it is relationships which give us the inspiration and the motivation to continue the journey.

I recently received a letter singing the praises of a new private school. Letters like this appear in my mailbox with some frequency, and I always read them with interest. They give me reason to pause and reflect upon our educational choices. Why do we continue to educate our children at home?

When we began, our reasons were largely academic: one-on-one tutoring is an excellent method of education and it yields academically excellent results. As we continued our journey, we began to notice the spiritual fruits of keeping our children home. They were learning their faith day in and day out alongside adults who have a vested interest in their eternal well-being.

Today, though, I see another blessing of home education. Today, my fifth grader, Michael, is upstairs reading a fine historical novel. When he is finished, he will discuss it with me and we will enjoy the nuances of the story together. Then, he will probably choose to illustrate it, as drawing is his passion. Home education will ensure he has plenty of time for these pursuits.

He is listening to Mozart as he reads. Lately, he has done research, which leads him to believe that Mozart is good for his brain. That may be so, but the reason he is listening to Mozart today is that this is the CD preferred by his baby brother, Stephen.

Michael, is reading, propped up on my bed with Stephen draped across his chest. Stephen is sound asleep, taking labored, wheezing breaths through his open mouth. The baby is sick, and we have discovered that the only way he will sleep is if someone holds him upright. This morning, Michael volunteered to hold his brother for as long as he would sleep.

In the steamy room, to the music of Mozart and the undertones of the humidifier, my sons are forging an incredible bond. Stephen is learning that Michael is a source of comfort and refuge when he is needy. Stephen is blessed. Michael is learning to comfort, to soothe, and to serve. He is learning that whatever he does to his little brothers, he does to his Lord. Michael is blessed. For both boys, this is a blessing of untold magnitude.

This morning, as he reads, Michael will learn something about Harriet Tubman. He will learn something about Mozart. But he will learn more about compassion. This morning's lessons are in history, music, and life. This fifth-grader will know about slavery and sonatas. He will also know strength and sacrifice. He will learn that lesson as his arms grow weary, his chest becomes damp, and he tires of sitting so long in one position. He'll shift ever so gently, but he won't put that baby down and he won't call for me to come get him.

I know he won't because this child has shown me time and time again that he understands what it is to serve someone younger or weaker or sicker. Michael continually puts the needs of his younger siblings ahead of his own wants. Many of his lessons in the past couple of years have been lessons in service. As he has served, he has discovered what love really is. He has learned those lessons here at home, largely during traditional school hours.

They weren't written into my plan books; their success won't be measured on a standardized test in May. They aren't contrived "service hours" projects, required for promotion. They are real, relevant, unselfish acts of love which originate in the heart of a child.

These lessons will bear fruit for generations to come. These "life lessons" will shape the man Michael is becoming. They will shape the husband and father he may be. They are forming a remarkable brother and son. I could not have imagined this facet of our educational plan when we made the decision to educate our children at home. It is an unexpected blessing that has brought us great joy.

We continue to educate our children at home because of the freedom to choose excellent books which stir children's hearts and inspire their souls. We continue to educate our children at home because here we are able to surround them with fine music and lovely art all day long. And we continue to educate our children at home because here an eleven-year-old boy can cradle a sick baby and learn the lesson of a rare and lasting love.

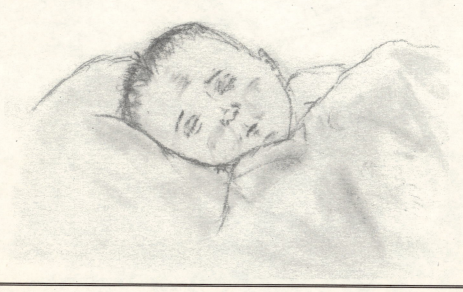

Read Around the Year Booklist

I was very hesitant to include a booklist. By their very nature, lists are limited. Fortunately, good literature is limitless. However, we have to begin to choose somewhere. This list is intended to be such a beginning. With the list below, the parent educator can apply the principles outlined in this book. She can begin to craft and to plan a curriculum tailored for her children. The list is designed to offer both structure and freedom.

In the third- through eighth-grade years, care was taken to include at least one living science book and one saint's biography or book of a spiritual nature in each month. At least one book in every month is marked with an asterisk to indicate a science theme. Books which are saints' stories or spiritual reading are marked with a cross. Most can, and should, be read aloud to the entire family. Everyone can benefit from them. As much as possible, saints' stories are organized according to feast days or historical themes.

All of these books open doors to further inquiry. Each month is a loosely organized, self-contained study. It is up to the discretion of the parent educator to decide whether or not to use all the books in any given month. For some books, the child will only read and narrate. For others, you may spend the entire month (or more) exploring further the themes presented. Don't rush; give the child plenty of time to dwell on the subject and to make connections. Allow him time and space to become intimate with the authors and the characters. Perhaps you will plan to cover this booklist in ten years, instead of nine.

Remember, this is a booklist, not a curriculum. You will write the curriculum. I think it would be impossible to adequately cover every book listed for any given year. There are many, many choices here. There are also many books which are not on the list but which would make excellent food for thought. The books here are rich and varied; great springboards for all sorts of interesting studies. A Book of Centuries and a Science Notebook will be necessary organizing tools to help bring the big picture into clear focus.

Philosophical Resources

Charlotte Mason's Original Homeschooling Series (Mason)

A Charlotte Mason Companion (Andreola)

Educating the WholeHearted Child (Clarkson)

Wild Days (Rackliffe)

A Charlotte Mason Study Guide (Gardner)

How to Home School (Graham)

Natural Structure (Walsh)

The Good Shepherd and the Child (Cavalletti)

A Landscape with Dragons (O'Brien)

Resources for Research and Answering the Inevitable Children's Questions

The Holy Bible, Revised Standard Version

Catechism of the Catholic Church

The Harp and Laurel Wreath (Berquist)

The Kingfisher History Encyclopedia

A History of US, volumes 1–11 (Hakim)

A Child's History of the World (Hillyer)

Christ the King Lord of History (Carroll)

The Kingfisher Science Encyclopedia

An assortment of field guides

Handbook of Nature Study (Comstock)

National Geographic magazine

National Geographic United States Atlas for Young Explorers (National Geographic Society)

National Geographic World Atlas for Young Explorers (National Geographic Society)

Butler's Lives of the Saints

Saints of the Church: A Teacher's Guide to the Vision Books (Allen)

Sister Wendy's Story of Painting (Beckett)

The DK Art School series (Dorling Kindersley)

Resources For Further Study

As I have explored the themes in the following books with my children, certain resources have proven helpful time and time again. While this is just a short list and by no means exhaustive, it is nice to have these books readily available to answer questions and provide further food for thought. As with any reference books available, discretion must be used to weed out objectionable presentations of the facts. That is all part of the learning experience!

Booklists, by their very nature, change. For a current version of this list, please visit www.4reallearning.com and click on "suggestions toward a curriculum."

Primary
Kindergarten through Second Grade

Stories for Narration: The child narrates orally and Mom keyboards and prints. The child illustrates and the narrations are gathered into a book:

Kindergarten: *The Beginner's Bible* (Henley)
First Grade: *The Children's Book of Virtues, The Children's Book of America, The Children's Book of Heroes, The Children's Book of Faith* (Bill Bennett, Michael Hague)
Second Grade: *Sister Wendy's Book of Saints* (Beckett), *Once Upon a Time Saints* (Pochocki), *More Once Upon a Time Saints* (Pochocki)

Any of the following three lists can be used with children who are in kindergarten through second grade.

Primary Cycle A

September
<u>Illustrator Michael Hague</u>
The 23rd Psalm
The Velveteen Rabbit
Aesop's Fables
Alphabears

October
<u>Audrey Wood</u>
Little Mouse, The Red Ripe Strawberry...
The Napping House
Balloonia
Silly Sally

November
When I Was Young in the Mountains (Rylant)
Appalachia (Rylant)
The Rag Coat (Mills)
N. C. Wyeth's Pilgrim's (San Souci)
Beginning of the de Paola Christmas unit discussed in Chapter Seven

December
De Paola Christmas unit

January
End of de Paola Christmas unit
A New Coat for Anna (Ziefert)
Owl Moon (Yolen)
Stopping By Woods on a Snowy Evening (Frost/Jeffers)
Bear (Schoenherr)

February
Allen Say
Grandfather's Journey
Under the Cherry Blossom Tree
Emma's Rug
Allison
The Bicycle Man
Tea with Milk
How My Parents Learned to Eat

March
Eric Carle
The Very Hungry Caterpillar
The Grouchy Ladybug
The Very Lonely Firefly
The Very Quiet Cricket

April
Beatrix Potter
The Complete Tales of Peter Rabbit

May
Miss Rumphius (Cooney)
Storm in the Night (Stolz)
All Those Secrets of the World (Yolen)
Mirette on the High Wire (McCully)
Mirette and Bellini Cross Niagara Fall (McCully)

June
Peter Spier
The Star-Spangled Banner
Circus!
People
Noah's Ark

July/ August
Robert McClosky
Blueberries for Sal
Lentil
Make Way for Ducklings
Time of Wonder
One Morning in Maine
Burt Dow, Deep Water Man

Primary Cycle B

September
Duffy and the Devil comical version of Rumpelstiltskin (Zemach)
Rapunzel (Zelinsky)
The Sleeping Beauty (Schart Hyman)
Little Red Riding Hood (Schart Hyman)

October
Goldilocks and the Three Bears (Brett)
Thumbelina (Jeffers)
Snow White and the Seven Dwarfs (Jarell/Burkert)
Snow White and Rose Red (Cooney)
Cinderella (Marcia Brown)
The Three Billy Goats Gruff (Galdone)

November
Fables (Lobel)
The Aesop for Children (Winter)

December
The Miracle of Saint Nicholas (Whelan)
The Donkey's Dream (Berger)
The Legend of the Candy Cane (Walburg)
Polar Express (Van Allsburg)
Christmas Trolls (Brett)

January
<u>Jan Brett</u>
The Mitten
Fritz and the Beautiful Horses
Trouble with Trolls
Town Mouse, Country Mouse
The First Dog

February
Snowy Day (Keats)
Warm as Wool (Sanders)
Katy and the Big Snow (Burton)
Daniel's Duck (Bulla)

March
Hush Little Baby (Zemach)
Hush Little Baby (Aliki)
Hush Little Baby (Long)
All the Pretty Horses (Jeffers)
London Bridge Is Falling Down (Spier)

April
<u>Max Lucado</u>
Just in Case You Ever Wonder
The Crippled Lamb
Because I Love You
You Are Special

May
Zin! Zin! Zin! A Violin (Moss)
Stone Soup (Brown)
Drummer Hoff (Emberley)
Saint George and the Dragon (Hodges)

June
Thy Friend, Obadiah (Turkle)
The Chanticleer and the Fox (Cooney)
Madeline (Bemelmans)
Rain Makes Applesauce (Scheer)

July
The Story About Ping (Flack/Wiese)
At the Beach/In the Park/ In the Snow (Huy Vuon Lee)
Lon Po Po (Young)
Five Chinese Brothers (Bishop/Wiese)
Maples in the Mist (Minfong Ho)

August
Johnny Appleseed (Kellogg)
John Henry (Keats)
Story of Paul Bunyan (Emberley)
Pecos Bill (Kellogg)
Brer Rabbit and His Tricks (Gorey)

Primary Cycle C

September
<u>Jill Barklem: Brambly Hedge</u>
Autumn Story
Spring Story
Sea Story
The High Hills

October
How to Make An Apple Pie and See The World (Priceman)
The Complete Tales of Winnie the Pooh (Milne)
<u>de Paola: Saint Stories</u>
Francis
Patrick
Christopher

November
<u>Gerald McDermott</u>
Arrow to the Sun
Coyote
Daniel O'Rourke
Papagayo

December
A Christmas Story (Wildsmith)
This is the Star (Dunbar)
How the Grinch Stole Christmas (Seuss)
The Legend of the Christmas Rose (Hooks)

January
Oh, A-Hunting We Will Go (Langstaff)
Frog Went A Courtin' (Rojankovsky)
Clementine (Quackenbush)
Go Tell Aunt Rhody (Aliki)
Skip to My Lou (Westcott)

February
Mufaro's Beautiful Daughters (Steptoe)
Why Mosquitoes Buzz in People's Ears (Aardema/Dillon)
Ashanti to Zulu: African Traditions (Musgrove)
Jambo Means Hello (Feelings)

March
<u>Joanne Ryder</u>
White Bear, Ice Bear
Catching the Wind
Chipmunk Song
My Father's Hands

April
Benjamin's Box (Carlson)
The Tale of Three Trees (Hunt)
Petook: An Easter Story (Houselander)
Does God Know How to Tie His Shoes? (Carlstrom)

May
<u>Arnold Lobel</u>
Frog and Toad series
On Market Street
Mouse Tales

June
<u>Molly Bang</u>
The Grey Lady and the Strawberry Snatcher
Ten, Nine, Eight
When Sophie Gets Angry—Really, Really Angry
Goose

July
<u>Charlotte Zolotow</u>
Mr. Rabbit and the Lovely Present
I Like to Be Little
Do You Know What I'll Do?
Over and Over

August
<u>Joy Hulme</u>
What If?: Just Wondering Poems
Bubble Trouble
Sea Squares
Sea Sums

Elementary
Third Grade through Sixth Grade

Elementary Cycle A

September

Animal Stories

James Herriot Treasury for Children (Herriot)
Just So Stories (Kipling)
The Wind in the Willows (Grahame)
The Book of Dragons (Hague)
+*Children of Fatima* (Windeatt)

October

E.B. White

* *Charlotte's Web*
* *Stuart Little*
* *Trumpet of the Swan*
+*The Little Flower* (Windeatt)

November

Colonial America

Courage of Sarah Noble (Dagliesh)
The Matchlock Gun (Edmonds)
Mr. Revere and I (Lawson)
A Lion To Guard Us (Bulla)
* *One Small Square: Woods* (Silver)
+*The Miraculous Medal* (Windeatt)

December

The Huron Carol (Tyrell)
The Christmas Candle (Evans)
The Littlest Angel (Tazewell)
The Christmas Miracle of Jonathon Toomey (Wojciechowski)
Christmas in Noisy Village (Lindgren)

January/ February

* The Little House Series (Wilder)
  Little House in the Big Woods
  Little House on the Prairie
  On The Banks of Plum Creek
  By the Shores of Silver Lake
  The Long Winter
  Little Town on the Prairie
  Farmer Boy
  The Martha Years Series (Wiley)
  The Charlotte Years Series (Wiley)
+*Pauline Jaricot* (Windeatt)
+*St. Elizabeth's Three Crowns* (Thompson)

[240]

March
<u>Marguerite Henry</u>
* *Misty of Chincoteague*
* *Stormy, Misty's Foal*
* *Justin Morgan Had a Horse*
* *King of the Wind*
+*St. Martin de Porres* (Windeatt)

April
<u>Westward Expansion</u>
The Cabin Faced West (Fritz)
On to Oregon (Morrow)
* *Tree in the Trail* (Holling)
+*St. Louis de Montfort* (Windeatt)

May
<u>Southern Studies</u>
Phoebe the Spy (Griffin)
* *Minn of the Mississippi* (Holling)
Turn Homeward, Hannalee (Beatty)
Be Ever Hopeful, Hannalee (Beatty)
+*Patron Saint of First Communicants* (Windeatt)

June
<u>Sea Adventures</u>
Pippi Longstocking (Lindgren)
* *We Didn't Mean to go to Sea* (Ransome)
* *Seabird* (Holling)
* *Pagoo* (Holling)
* *One Small Square: Seashore* (Silver)
+*St. John Masias* (Windeatt)

July
<u>Frances Hodgson Burnett</u>
* *The Secret Garden*
A Little Princess
Little Lord Fauntleroy
+*For the Children* (John Paul II)

August
<u>Victorian Fancy</u>
Peter Pan (Barrie)
Alice in Wonderland (Carroll)
The Jungle Books (Kipling)
The Princess and Curdie (MacDonald)
* *One Small Square: Pond* (Silver)
+*St. Rose of Lima* (Windeatt)

[241]

Elementary Cycle B

September
<u>Anne Pellowski</u>
First Farm in the Valley: Anna's Story
Winding Valley Farm: Annie's Story
Stairstep Farm: Anna Rose's Story
Willow Wind Farm: Betsy's Story
Betsy's Up and Down Year
+*Prayer* (Biffi)

October/November
The Chronicles of Narnia series, 7 titles
    (C.S. Lewis)
* *Autumn Across America* (Simon)
* *One Small Square: Night Sky* (Silver)
+*Francis and Clare, Saints of Assisi* (Homan)

December
The Way to Bethlehem (Biffi)
Christmas with Anne and Other Holiday
    Stories (Montgomery)
The Best Christmas Pageant Ever (Robinson)
The Night Before Christmas (Moore/Tudor)

January/February
<u>Edgar and Ingri d'Aulaire</u>
Pocahontas
George Washington
Benjamin Franklin
Buffalo Bill
Abe Lincoln
* *Ben and Me* (Lawson)
* *Mountain Born* (Yates)
+*St. Thomas Aquinas* (Windeatt)
+*St. Isaac and the Indians* (Lomask)

March
<u>The Letzenstein Chronicles</u> (Meriol Trevor)
Crystal Snowstorm
Following the Phoenix
Angel and Dragon
Rose and Crown
* *Kildee House* (Montgomery)
+*St. Catherine of Siena* (Windeatt)

April
<u>The Anne of Green Gables Series</u>
    <u>(Montgomery)</u>
* *Anne of Green Gables*
Anne of Avonlea
Chronicles of Avonlea
Anne of the Island
+*The Sacraments* (Biffi)

May/June	**July/August**
<u>Gene Stratton-Porter</u>	<u>Arthur Ransome</u>

May/June

<u>Gene Stratton-Porter</u>
* *Girl of the Limberlost*
* *Keeper of the Bees*
* *The Harvester*
* *Freckles*
* *Michael O'Halloran*
* *Laddie: A True Blue Story*
+*St. Margaret Mary Alacoque and the Promises of the Sacred Heart of Jesus* (Windeatt)
+*The Ten Commandments* (Biffi)

July/August

<u>Arthur Ransome</u>
* *Swallows and Amazons*
* *Swallowdale*
* *The Pigeon Post*
* *The Coot Club*
* *The Big Six*
+*Saint Benedict* (Windeatt)
+*Saint Dominic* (Windeatt)

Elementary Cycle C

September
<u>Ireland</u>
<u>The Bantry Bay Series</u> (von Stockum)
The Cottage At Bantry Bay
Francie on the Run
Pegeen
Red Hugh, Prince of Donegal (Reilly)
* *One Small Square: Backyard* (Silver)
+*St Therese and the Roses* (Homan)

October
<u>Vikings</u>
Beorn the Proud (Polland)
Sword Song (Sutcliff)
Nordic Gods and Heroes (Colum)
+*Brendan The Navigator* (Fritz)
One Small Square: Swamp (Silver)

November
<u>Sea Exploration</u>
Leif the Lucky (d'Aulaire)
Christopher Columbus (d'Aulaire)
All Set Sail (Sperry)
Around the World in a Hundred Years (Fritz)
* *Ship* (Macaulay)
* *One Small Square: Coral Reef* (Silver)
+*St. Francis of the Seven Seas* (Nevins)

December
Letters from Father Christmas (Tolkien)
Winter Holiday (Ransome)
A Christmas Memory (Capote)

January
<u>The Arctic Circle</u>
* *Stone Fox* (Gardiner)
* *Water Sky* (George)
* *Gentle Ben* (Morey)
* *Snow Dog* (Kjelgaard)
* *One Small Square: Arctic Tundra* (Silver)
+ *My Path to Heaven* (Bliss)

February
<u>Classic Young United States</u>
Johnny Tremain (Forbes)
Caddie Woodlawn (Brink)
Sign of the Beaver (Speare)
Sarah, Plain and Tall (MacLachan)
* *Exploring the Earth With John Wesley Powell* (Elsohn Ross)
+*St. Francis Solano* (Windeatt)

March
<u>Native Americans</u>
* *Black Star, Bright Dawn* (O'Dell)
  Sing Down the Moon (O'Dell)
* *Island of the Blue Dolphins* (O'Dell)
  The Light in the Forest (Richter)
+*The Man Who Founded California* (Murville)
+*Kateri Tekakwitha* (Brown)

April
<u>Brian Jacques</u>
* *Redwall*
* *Mossflower*
* *Martin the Warrior*
* *The Legend of Luke*
* *One Small Square: Cave* (Silver)
+*The Apostles Creed* (Biffi)

May
<u>Dog Stories</u>
* *Big Red* (Kjelgaard)
* *Old Yeller* (Gipson)
* *Call of the Wild* (London)
* *A Dog of Flanders* (Oui'da)
+*Saint Bernadette* (Pauli)

June/July/August
<u>Louisa May Alcott</u>
Little Women
Little Men
Jo's Boy's
Eight Cousins
Rose in Bloom
An Old Fashioned Girl
Jack and Jill
Invincible Louisa (Meigs)
+*The Cure of Ars* (Windeatt)

Upper Elementary
Sixth Grade through Eighth Grade

Upper Elementary Cycle A

September

Early Middle Ages

The Story of Rolf and the Viking Bow (French)
Beowulf the Warrior (Serraillier)
+*Augustine Came to Kent* (Willard)
Son of Charlemagne (Willard)

October

High Middle Ages

Adam of the Road (Gray)
+*If All the Swords in England* (Willard)
+*The Hidden Treasure of Glaston* (Jewett)
The Red Keep (French)
* *Cathedral* (Macauley)

November

Shakespeare

Tales from Shakespeare (Lamb)
Taming of the Shrew (Shakespeare)
Midsummer Night's Dream (Shakespeare)
William Shakespeare and the Globe (Aliki)
The Bard of Avon (Stanley)
Brush Up Your Shakespeare (MacRone)
+*Edmund Campion, Hero of God's Underground* (Gardiner)
* *The New Way Things Work* (Macauley) Part 1

December

Just David (Porter)
The Christmas Tree (Salamon)
The Bronze Bow (Speare)
The Trumpeter of Krakow (Kelly)

January

Genevieve Foster

The World of Captain John Smith
George Washington's World
* *Science Discoveries: Isaac Newton and Gravity* (Parker)
* *The New Way Things Work* (Macaulay) Part 2
+*Mother Cabrini: Missionary to the World* (Keyes)

February

Tales from Other Cultures

Star of Light (St. John),
Born in the Year of Courage (Crofford)
The Samurai's Tale (Haugard)
The Good Master (Seredy)
Commodore Perry in the Land of the Shogun (Blumberg)
+*St. Philip of the Joyous Heart* (Connolly)
+*Mother Teresa: In My Own Words* (Mother Teresa)
+*Mother Teresa* (Chawla)
* *The New Way Things Work* (Macaulay) Part 3

March
China
- *Dragonwings* (Yep)
- *Dragon's Gate* (Yep)
- *Young Fu of the Upper Yangtze* (Lewis)
- + *Mission to Cathay* (Polland)
- * *The New Way Things Work* (Macaulay) Part 4

April
Joan Aiken
- * *Wolves of Willoughby Chase*
- * *Nightbirds on Nantucket*
- * *Black Hearts in Battersea*
- +*Saint Anthony and the Christ Child* (Homan)

May
World War I
- *After the Dancing Days* (Rostkowski)

The Mitchells series (Hilda Von Stockum)
- *The Mitchells: Five For Victory*
- *Canadian Summer*
- *Friendly Gables*
- +*St. Hyacinth of Poland* (Windeatt)
- * *Rascal* (North)

June
World War II
- *The Endless Steppe* (Hautzig)
- *The Winged Watchman* (Von Stockum)
- *The Borrowed House* (Von Stockum) [for more mature readers]
- *The Small War of Sergeant Donkey* (Daly)
- +*The Hiding Place* (ten Boom)
- * *The New Way Things Work* (Macaulay) Eureka!

July
Ancient Greece
- * *Archimedes and the Door of Science* (Bendick)
- *A Wonder Book for Girls and Boys* (Hawthorne)
- *d'Aulaire's Book of Greek Myths* (d'Aulaire)
- *The Children's Homer* (Colum)
- +*King David and his Songs* (Windeatt)

August
Early Empires
- *Tales of the Greek Heroes* (Green)
- *Black Ships Before Troy* (Sutcliff)
- *The Wanderings of Odysseus* (Sutcliff)
- *Between the Forest and the Hills* (Lawrence)
- *Ides of April* (Ray)
- +*Fingal's Quest* (Polland)
- * *City* (Macaulay)
- * *Exploring Planet Earth* (Tiner)

[247]

Upper Elementary Cycle B

September
<u>George MacDonald and C.S. Lewis</u>
Wise Woman and Other Stories (MacDonald)
+*Screwtape Letters* (Lewis)
+*Abolition of Man* (Lewis)
Till We Have Faces (Lewis)
* *My Friend Flicka* (O'Hara)

October
<u>Chesterton</u>
The Man Who Was Thursday
The Best of Father Brown
+*Heretics and Orthodoxy*
* *Northern Farm: A Glorious Year on a Small Maine Farm* (Beston)

November
<u>J.R.R. Tolkien</u>
The Hobbit
The Fellowship of the Ring
* *Owls in the Family* (Mowat)
+*Saint John Bosco and Saint Dominic Savio* (Beebe)

December
The Christmas Box (Evans)
Sir Gawain and the Green Knight (Tolkien)
Papa's Angels (Paxton)

January
<u>Egypt</u>
Mara, Daughter of the Nile (McGraw)
The Golden Goblet (McGraw)
Tales of Ancient Egypt (Green)
The Cat of the Bubastes (Henty)
+*Mother Seton and the Sisters of Charity* (Power-Waters)
* *Cat Mummies* (Trumble)
Pyramid (Macaulay)

February
<u>Rosemary Sutcliff</u>
* *Outcast*
* *The Eagle of the Ninth*
* *The Silver Branch*
* *The Lantern Bearers*
+*St Paul the Apostle: The Story of the Apostle to the Gentiles* (Windeatt)

March
<u>Courage</u>
Kon-Tiki (Heyerdahl)
* *Swiss Family Robinson* (Wyss)
Call It Courage (Sperry)
Onion John (Krumgold)
* *Pilgrim at Tinker Creek* (Dillard)
+*An Introduction to the Liturgical Year* (Biffi)

April
<u>France</u>
Les Miserables (Hugo)
The Song at the Scaffold (le Fort)
The Scarlet Pimpernel (Orczy)
In Search of Honor (Hess)
* *Fabre's Book of Insects* (Fabre)
+*Cure of Ars* (Lomask)

May
<u>Showell Styles</u>
The Midshipman Quinn Collection (Styles)
* *The Yearling* (Rawlings)
+*Set All Afire* (de Wohl)
+*Saint Ignatius and the Company of Jesus* (Derleth)

June
<u>Jean Craighead George</u>
* *My Side of the Mountain*
* *On the Far Side of the Mountain*
* *Julie of the Wolves*
+*Saint Dominic and the Rosary* (Beebe)

July
<u>Mark Twain</u>
Huckleberry Finn
Tom Sawyer
The Prince and the Pauper
+*Joan of Arc*
* *Rocket Boys: A Memoir* (Hickam)

August
<u>Civil War</u>
Rifles For Watie (Keith)
The Red Badge of Courage (Crane)
Wait For Me, Watch for Me Eula Bee (Beatty)
Across Five Aprils (Hunt)
* *They Loved to Laugh* (Worth)
+*Saint Pius X* (Diethelm)

Upper Elementary Cycle C

September
Robert Louis Stevenson
Treasure Island
Kidnapped
The Black Arrow
Flint's Island (Wibberley)
+*Francis of Assisi* (Chesterton)
* *Darwin on Trial* (Johnson)

October
Bronte and Austen
Wuthering Heights (Bronte)
Jane Eyre (Bronte)
Pride and Prejudice (Austen)
+*Surprised by Truth* (Madrid)
* *Life's Matrix: A Biography of Water* (Ball) [This contains evolutionary content. Read after *Darwin on Trial* and discuss.]
Eyewitness: Chemistry (Newmark)

November
Charles Dickens
Great Expectations
Oliver Twist
The Tale of Two Cities
+*Blessed Margaret of Castello* (Bonniwell)
* *Antoine Lavoisier: Science, Administration, and Revolution* (Donovan)
Eyewitness: Chemistry (Newmark)

December
Dickens
Cricket on the Hearth
Christmas Stories

January/February
Howard Pyle:
Otto of the Silver Hand
The Story of King Arthur and His Knights
The Story of the Champions of the Round Table
The Story of Sir Lancelot and his Champions
The Story of the Grail and the Passing of Arthur
The Merry Adventures of Robin Hood
+*The Great Heresies* (Belloc)
+*The Citadel of God* (deWohl)
* *Galileo's Daughter* (Sobel)
* *Castle* (Macaulay)

March
Canada
With Pipe, Paddle and Song (Yates)
Madeline Takes Command (Brill)
Calico Captive (Speare)
+*Father Marquette and the Great Rivers* (Derleth)
* *Incident at Hawk's Hill* (Eckert)

April
Colonial America/Revolutionary War
Reb and the Redcoats (Savery)
* *Carry On, Mr. Bowditch* (Latham)
* *Diary of an Early American Boy* (Sloane)
Witch of Blackbird Pond (Speare)
+*Our Lady of Guadalupe & the Conquest of Darkness* (Carroll)

May
Coming of Age
Under a Changing Moon (Benary-Isbert)
The Rose Round (Trevor)
* *The Tracker* (Brown, Jr.)
* *The Search* (Brown, Jr.)
+*The Song of Bernadette* (Werfel)

June
World War II
The Diary of Anne Frank (Frank)
The Borrowed House (Von Stockum)
The Story of the Trapp Family Singers (Von Trapp)
Escape From Warsaw (Serraillier)
+*Forget Not Love: The Passion of Saint Maximillian Kolbe* (Frossard)
* *Madame Curie: A Biography* (Curie) [Includes a brief description of Mme. Curie leaving the faith after her mother dies.]

July
Modern Church Inspiration
+*Witness to Hope* (Weigel)
+*Edith Stein* (Herbstrith)
+*We're on a Mission from God* (Bonacci)
* *Walden* (Thoreau)
* *The Outermost House: A Year of Life on the Great Beach of Cape Cod* (Beston)

August
James Herriot
All Creatures Great and Small
All Things Bright and Beautiful
All Things Wise and Wonderful
The Lord God Made Them All
Lyrical Life Science Volume Three: The Human Body (Eldon)
The Anatomy Coloring Book (Kapit) [Use a razor knife to remove objectionable pages.]
+*Story of a Soul* (Therese of Lisieux, John Clarke translation)

Children's Art Credits

The children's art throughout this book was created over a period of several years. Each age listed here corresponds to the chid's age at the time the drawing was made.

page 16	House	Courtney Kampa	age 10
page 23	Flowers	Michael Foss	age 13
page 33	Nature Journal Page	Michael Foss	age 11
page 43	Coffee Pot & Cup with Roses	Michael Foss	age 13
page 86	Christian Camping	Keenan Kampa	age 13
page 89	Stone Wall at Gettysburg	Patrick Foss	age 8
page 98	Spider	Mary Beth Foss	age 6
page 102	Nature Journal Page	Michael Foss	age 11
page 118	Holy Family	Michael Foss	age 13
page 122	Girl Praying	Michael Foss	age 13
page 123	Teacup	Keenan Kampa	age 13
page 130	Mother Teresa	Renata See	age 16
page 138	Coffee Pot & Fruit	Keenan Kampa	age 12
page 144	Ballerina	Keenan Kampa	age 13
page 148	Ballerina	Mary Beth Foss	age 6
page 154	Ballet Slippers	Michael Foss	age 13
page 165	Pope John Paul II	Michael Foss	age 13
page 166	Girl with Ball	Renata See	age 16
page 169	Brothers: Christian & Patrick	Renata See	age 16
page 170	Saint Therese	Keenan Kampa	age 12
page 174	Paddy Playing Soccer	Mary Beth Foss	age 6
page 180	Karol Wojtyla	Michael Foss	age 13
page 181	Ball & Glove	Keenan Kampa	age 13
pages 184–185	Soccer Ball & Sneaker	Michael Foss	age 13
page 204	Praying Hands	Renata See	age 16
page 209	Pumpkin	Michael Foss	age 13
page 216	Plums	Renata See	age 16
page 226	Sleeping with Baby	Keenan Kampa	age 13
page 229	Baby Sleeping	Michael Foss	age 13
page 230	Dad Reading	Keenan Kampa	age 13

Notes